THE POWER
THAT WORKS WITHIN

Sermons for the
First Half of Pentecost
Series B

Leonard W. Mann

THE POWER THAT WORKS WITHIN

ISBN 0-89536-492-1

CONTENTS

AN INTRODUCTORY WORD

Now to him who by the power at work within us is able to do far more abundantly than all that we ask or think, to him be glory in the church and in Christ Jesus to all generations, for ever and ever. Amen.

Here, recorded in Ephesians 3:20, we have one of the majestic doxologies of the Apostle Paul. It speaks excitedly of a power that is at work within us. The Apostle is quite aware, as we should be, that we do not have to walk or work alone. God does not leave us to the limitations of our own resources, unaided, unhelped.

I still remember the first and only swimming lesson I ever had. It was given to me by my father. One summer day he took me to the old swimming hole where the water of Indian Creek ran deep and slow. He carried me out until the water was about waist deep to him, and there he laid me face-down on the surface of the water, his hand supporting underneath my midsection. Then he withdrew his hand, saying, "Now you're on your own!" That was the conclusion of the swimming lesson: It was swim or else! No, my father would never have permitted me to drown — but neither did he do much to help me swim.

God has a better way of dealing with us. Never does he turn his people loose, withdraw his hand and say, "Now you're on your own." He is with us; his power is at work within us. There is no doubt that Paul is speaking here of the working power of the Holy Spirit.

The disciples at Pentecost were unsure of their assignment, the signals were unclear to them, and they were ill-equipped for their task whatever it should prove to be. But the coming of the Spirit changed that, and the transformation was a spectacular one.

As we contemplate Pentecost, or preach or write of it, two areas of awareness press themselves upon us. First: what God is doing for us — by his Spirit. Second: what God is prompting and helping us to do for others — by his Spirit. These two insights are the theme of what follows.

They are the two most significant aspects of the presence of the Spirit with us. Some of these messages will deal with one of these, some with the other, and some with both. It is my hope that altogether they may make some contribution to the vigor and joy of Christian living and provide some encouragement for Christian serving.

This is now the third time I have written for The C.S.S. Publishing Company on a major theme of the Christian Faith. In 1977 it was the Advent and Christmas theme under the title *Stars*

You Never Saw Before. In 1980 it was the Easter theme under the title *God's East Wind.* I am pleased currently to write on the theme of Pentecost. I do not write of this as only a named date in ancient history, but mainly as an important day-to-day reality in the lives of all who would walk with Christ.

A Clinic in Life

Pentecost Sunday

"If anyone thirst, let him come . . . " — *John 7:37*

He walked the common roads where others had walked before and where yet others, coming after, have walked for almost 2,000 years. But the things he did and the things he said were different from the deeds and words of any other who ever walked those roads or any roads of this planet anywhere. In common terms he spoke of most uncommon things. To common people he said things never said before — or since, except when quoting him. He was Jesus: by this was he called; it was his common name. We know him as Christ, and so he is.

Many amazing things were said by him. One of these is written for us in Matthew 11:28: "Come to me, all who labor and are heavy-laden, and I will give you rest." "All," he said. There is a lot of laboring in the world, many heavy loads to bear. But he said, come to me, all of you. The invitation is enormous, virtually unthinkable. But the promise is more so: "I will give you rest." How? Who is he to say this? If I should say it, most would laugh, and if any should take me seriously about it, they would know me to be wrong, believe me demented perhaps. There is no record, though, that any laughed when Jesus said this. Many were perplexed, yes — and some still are. But not many are laughing even yet — as they would at me. He was different; they knew it then, and, deeply, we know it now.

Now here is this seventh chapter of John with its startling account of other amazing things which Jesus said. He went up to the temple at a time of high festival, at the very middle of the feast. And there the people, having heard him, said, "How is it this man has learning, when he has never studied?" Men who came to arrest him, returning to the authorities without him, were asked why. Their answer: "No man ever spoke like this man!" They were right about that — no man ever had. Moreover, no one else ever has, even yet, not with anything even remotely akin to credibility.

One of the things he said, confounding them: "If any one

thirst, let him come to me and drink." Nor did he whisper this to a few; he stood and shouted it to the multitude, he cried it out aloud, he proclaimed it to the vast crowds assembled there. The thirst of which he spoke, as they knew then and as we know now, was not a mere thirst for water, but was thirst of a spiritual kind. The drink which he offered was not mere water poured from a jar or gourd, but was a balm to assuage the parching pain of spirit which water alone can never reach. He offered himself as a limitless fountain at which thirsting humanity may find quenching for that thirst. And his offering is in such abundant measure that he declares that out of the heart of the person once thirsty shall come an overflowing stream, "rivers of living water."

One who is really listening cannot hear Jesus saying, "If anyone thirst, let him come to me and drink," without getting some sense that God in Christ is doing incredibly marvelous things for us. Incarnate in his Son, "God was in Christ reconciling the world to himself." (2 Corinthians 5:19) But this is a phenomenon which can never be relegated to past tense — he who was in Christ still is, and Christ says to all his people in all time and to us in our time, "I am with you." (Matthew 28:20) His reconciling ministry amongst us is not limited to a three-year space of ancient history.

Looking into a future that encompasses all time, Jesus said, "The Holy Spirit, whom the Father will send in my name, he will teach you all things, and bring to your remembrance all that I have said to you." (John 14:26) In a very real way, the coming of the Holy Spirit at Pentecost perpetuated and projected into all time the teaching, guiding, empowering ministrations of Christ to his people of Planet Earth. So whatever Christ was saying then is being said still. Let us hear it as a word freshly coming from his lips to our ears: "If any one thirst, let him come to me and drink."

Not only did Jesus say many amazing things, but it is remarkable also that in his time on earth many amazing things were said by others concerning him. One of these we may read in John 2:25: "He knew all men and needed no one to bear witness of man; for he himself knew what was in man."

Now let us consider all of this and what it can mean to us. We live in a day of extreme specialization, with work divided and subdivided into restricted segments, each with a definition uniquely its own. The trend is to know more and more about less and less. Perhaps in our age there is so much to know that no one person can know it all. The scope of human capability is so vast that no one person can cover it all. Take, for instance, the area of science, and, within this area, that of medical science. The specialties are legion. If your back aches, you go to one doctor; if your tummy hurts, you see another. If you have an earache, you go to a specialist in ears — perhaps depending on whether the problem is with your right ear or your left one! Well, not really — the specialization is not quite so minute, yet. But it's true, isn't it? Ours is a time of specialization, of high competence in narrow fields.

Let me put before you now an exciting truth: Jesus Christ is a SPECIALIST. He is a specialist in LIFE, our human life, our living. He understands the deep movements and surgings of the human spirit. He is the mastercraftsman of our race.

If your wristwatch won't run, you know where to take it. If a light switch won't work, you know whom to call. But what can you do when life goes wrong? All over the modern world, in great centers of population everywhere, are counseling centers, clinics for human problems. Here trained psychologists and psychiatrists maintain their trouble offices, here they probe the deep libidos of the human spirit and mind. Their signs are at their doors and windows and along the streets where they do their work. And there, within, these skilled people sit at polished desks meeting a parade of troubled persons who seek their aid.

To these specialized professionals come long lines of the broken, the beaten, the anxious, the confused, those for whom life has gone amiss, who somewhere along the journey have lost their way. Among these are the young, disillusioned already at their first encounters with living. There are the middle-aged, bewildered to know that the flush of youth is fading. There are the fully aged, some disappointed, some dissipated. There are the rich, having discovered their gold would not purchase what they had thought it would. And the poor — these are usually too poor to come.

And these people come in, they sit down, and they say, "Tell me, doctor, what is wrong and help me if you can." Sometimes some help is found and sometimes none.

Please forgive the personal reference now, but I must tell you this: I am a carpenter by trade. Before I was a minister, I worked at building and making things. Although I have been a minister of Christ for many years, I think of myself as a carpenter still. I am not ashamed of my trade: I know Another who was a carpenter — long ago in the village of Nazareth in Galilee.

What privilege would be mine should a messenger come to me one day, saying, "I am sent to commission you to make a sign, and you are to inscribe it thus: CLINIC IN LIFE — JESUS CHRIST, SPECIALIST."

I am sure I would set to work with a will. For the signboard I would select the best of materials, and I would build it sturdy and large. Then I would letter it bold. My hand, I suspect, would tremble a little, but I would do my best. And beneath the legend which I had inscribed I would append this subtitle: "If any one thirst, let him come to me and drink."

Then, the sign completed, I would like to hang it for him — somewhere along one of the main thoroughfares of the world where the streams of humanity pass. I would hang it high, for all to see. Then, his sign in place, if I could have the privilege, I would like to be his doorkeeper. Just that, his doorkeeper. I would like to stand there and invite the people as they pass that way. I would like to have them come, and then to usher them in — and softly close the door. There, with him alone, I would like them to say, "Tell me, Great Physician, what is wrong and please help me if you can."

What would he say? to you? to me? What would his answer be? Of course, I cannot know — I am only his doorkeeper, you see. In what way he would express his care, make his compassion known to you, I can but dimly guess, for I do not know you well enough, but he does. By what means he would reach out his love to you I cannot know, but I know he would.

But I do know something of what he would say to you, or to anyone. Some things are clear from what he has said already. The New Testament record of what he said in that time is enough to let us know where Jesus stands in relation to the way we live out our lives. We are given considerable insight as to how we should spend ourselves, use up our energies, act out our years. Whatever else Jesus might say to any one in particular, it is quite apparent that there are certain things he would say to everyone in general. So, perhaps, I do know a little of what he might say to you.

I know, for instance, that Jesus stands forever against all cheapening of our human life. To use life as though it were a dime-store trinket rather than a precious jewel is a use which Christ deplores. Understanding the spiritual character of what we are, he knows better than any other the awesome worth of a human life. He tells us clearly that even if one should gain the entire world and lose oneself, forfeit one's life, the deal would be a bad one (Mark 8:36; Luke 9:25). Sparrows are sold for pennies and farthings, and even they are precious in God's sight; but "you," said Jesus, are of infinitely greater value than many sparrows (Matthew 10:29-31; Luke 12:6-7). Jesus insists that "life is more than" food or clothing or sundry other things we may have thought it was (Matthew 6:25; Luke 12:23).

But to see the enormous worth of life most clearly, we must see it in the light of what happens at Calvary. Here God is so loving the world that "whosoever will" may believe and receive and have the kind of life that will never end (John 3:16). Many years ago a cynical philosopher wrote: "I would gladly have died for man, had I not rather suspected that man was not worth it." Jesus takes no such attitude toward us; he sees in us what is worth dying for.

Our measure of human worth is too often limited to the value of a man or woman in the labor market, the business world, or the military machine. But our Lord knows we are of greater worth; he alone really understands what any human person is and what that person may become. If we have entertained too little thoughts of what we are, let us recapture this truth and hold it firm: We are the very creatures that the all-wise and infinite God has chosen and delighted to set his love upon. For reasons of his own, God believes in us, and therefore gives his best for us, everlastingly loves, patiently endures our follies, trustfully awaits the day when these soiled gem-stones will catch at last the gleaming of his sun.

The most tragic of our folly has been committed when we have lost view of what we are, have thought of ourselves as merely biological, have disassociated ourselves from our spiritual selfhood. In the Grecian academy of Plato, the philosopher, no doubt in a test of his students, once described man as a "two-legged animal without feathers." Diogenes went out, plucked the feathers from a cock, brought the cock in, held it up before the assembly, and said, "Behold Plato's man." Man can never be defined in physical terms alone. His distinguishing character is a quality of spirit. Each of us needs to understand a truth of which Paul spoke: "Do you not know that you are God's temple and that God's Spirit dwells in you?" (1 Corinthians 3:16) Such is your worth, my friend, such is your value as God knows it to be.

But what are you worth to you? How do you value yourself? Too many people wear two tags. One represents the real worth of the person, the tag God has placed there. The other was put there by the person him/herself, and often it is a sign which says, "For sale cheap." The person is offering him/herself at a discount price, oblivious to the essential truth that life was never meant to be dispensed in anybody's bargain basement. Here, for example, is one who says, "I'm not too good" to do so-and-so. Well, I hope I am too good to do some types of things, and I hope you are. Someone writes, "Let it be said when life is through: Some things there were I would NOT do."

We are always devoting ourselves to something or other, and when that to which we give ourselves, that for which we let ourselves go, is unworthy or mean or low, then we are selling out too cheaply. Do you remember Judas, poor man? For thirty small coins he betrayed Christ, selling him, so Judas thought, into the hands of his enemies. But whom did Judas sell, really? Hester Cholmondeley gives the answer in these pointed lines:

Still, as of old, men by themselves are priced:
For thirty pieces Judas sold himself, not Christ.

If ever, my friend, you are tempted to meanly deal your life away, remember how big you are made, how great is your worth, to what heights you are designed to rise, how precious in the sight of God you are.

In the second place, I know also, for instance, that Jesus stands forever against all shallowness of our life. An animal is a prisoner of nature: a cat has a certain way of catching a mouse, wherever in the world. But a person can write a sonnet, sing a song, build a cathedral, lift eyes to the stars. We are creatures of infinite capacity, intended, as Paul suggests, to be "filled with all the fullness of God." (Ephesians 3:19) The dimensions of life accommodate deeps of spirit which are not to be ignored. But some do. They shut off the inner areas and burn to a crisp around the fringes. Their whole thrust of living is on levels that are superficial; they never let themselves live from the depths. Feverishly skimming froth from the surface of things, they never let themselves taste the elixir which bubbles in fountains underneath.

They are shallow, and our Lord is grieved that they are. More than anyone, he knows how much of life they are missing, what immense dimensions of life lie dormant deep within, what exciting potentials are covered and imprisoned there. Jesus would like us to know that "a man's life does not consist in the abundance of his possessions" (Luke 12:15) — or in the number of clubs joined or games played or miles traveled or places visited. These may be numbered among life's incidentals, but they are not life. Nor does one "live by bread alone" (Matthew 4:4) — nor by meat or milk or wine. A person has failed to comprehend what life is who presumes to live by its incidentals only.

And I know, too, in the third place, that Jesus stands forever against all narrowness of our life. He says, "Lift up your eyes and see." (John 4:35) It is good to see fields white for harvest; but there is much else also to be seen — broad vistas where life can expand in loving, serving, healing, and in venturing, reaching, climbing.

How easy it is to permit circumstances to fence us in, how easy to let some object nearby shut from our view the whole, vast dome of sky. How easy, too, it is to lose our perspective on reality and measure all things by some small segment of them, to strain out some small gnat and swallow a whole camel (Matthew 23:24). How inclined we are to zero in on the wrong things and lose our way, to lop off wide vistas of life and confine it to a rut. On a gravestone somewhere the epitaph reads this way: "Born a man; died a grocer." Born with infinite capacity for broad, rich, wholesome unfolding and development of manhood, but the man's life narrowed down — his interests, concerns, and efforts one by one were dropped along the way until only one was left. Of course, it is good to be a grocer, but the good groceryman should also be the man he was meant to be, having the range of love and reach of heart which belong to manhood at its best.

Knowing well our incessant peril of life's circumscription, Jesus gave us a formula for avoiding it: Seek first the Kingdom — and all these other things shall be yours as well (Matthew 6:33). Begin at the heart, the center, says Jesus, and round out your life from there. The life development which begins with the Kingdom at the center will never be fenced in by narrow walls that stop its growth at some early barricade. Put the Kingdom first, start from there, and the whole universe is yours to grow in. So, starting there, let heart go out, soul reach forth, mind stretch itself.

Well, in a general kind of way, I know this: Jesus, the Christ, stands forever against all the cheapening and the shallowness and the narrowness of our human life. But, better still, on the affirmative side, he offers us the glorious *alternative* of life that is total, full, and well-rounded. He calls us to new life in him. He understands our spiritual deeps that cry out to be reached and touched. He knows about our thirstings and promises us the water to quench them. He says, "The Son of Man is not come to destroy men's lives, but to save them." (Luke 9:56) He assures us that he has come so that we may have life, "and have it abundantly." (John 10:10) "If any one thirst, let him come to me and drink!"

He is saying: Here, give me that precious life of yours, and I will touch it, enrich, deepen, broaden it, and make it to abound as it is meant to do. Once he asked someone, "Do you believe that I am able to do this?" (Matthew 9:28) In answering, we need to be as confident of God as certain others of whom it is written that they were "fully persuaded that what he had promised he was able also to perform." (Romans 4:21 KJV) We need the assurance of Paul: "God is able to make all grace abound toward you" (2 Corinthians 9:8 KJV), and that he "is able to do far more abundantly than all that we ask or think" (Ephesians 3:20).

Your life in our Lord's hands is in able hands. And would you know how you can meet him, what his sign is, and where? His sign is not one that I made. His sign is the Cross — that instrument of death which he transformed into a symbol of life. And where is this? It is wherever your humble, penitent heart gives response to his great love.

The Adventure of Being Alive

The Holy Trinity

"You must be born anew . . ." — John 3:7

Have you observed how a baby grows? Growth is not merely a matter of gaining pounds and adding inches. There's more. The growing process is an adventure of experience and discovery. There comes, for example, the day when he finds his own hands and feet, discovering that they are his to command, that he can make them do things. He learns that he can insert his toes into his mouth, and so he does — as everyone stands about and smiles. He learns that he can make his hands caress his mother's face as she holds him close to her. More and more he becomes aware of the world around him, and more and more he reaches out to touch it. And the whole process begins with an event we call birth.

From the moment of this event, the child moves out into that series of events, following this, which we call living. In the normal process of growing, the child learns to experience the beauty of a rose, to feel the pulse of music, to sense the glory of a sunset. He identifies himself as part of a family and relates with other children at play and other boys and girls in his school. So does he come alive to the world of persons and things in the midst of which he is set.

The years pass, and this child becomes an adult, assuming a measure of responsibility among other human beings. He enters into relationship with them — in marriage and home, in his work, in his community. He involves himself in the struggle to shelter and feed and clothe himself and those for whom he cares. He is very much alive to the push and pull of the world around him; there is the incessant give and take between him and it. He is sensitive to its claims upon him, its offerings to him; he is well aware of the perils it presents, the hazards which are there. Having been born into a real and physical world, he is alive to the real and physical environment into which his birth has brought him.

But there is something more. Do not forget that he is man. He is not a pig, first sucking at the nipples of its mother sow, and then rooting in the earth for roots and worms. He is man: He can see the beauty of the rose which the pig cannot; he can thrill to the sound of music which the pig can never do; he can appreciate the magnificence of the sunset which the pig never can. He can put his mind to a task; he can write a poem, span a river with a bridge, or send a space ship to the stars.

He is man, and, being so, he is person. He is person as God is person — human person, to be sure, while God is divine, but person nevertheless. More than animal merely, he is spirit; as God is spirit, so is he. He has a body; it is his, his means of communicating with the real and physical world in which he lives. It is not accurate to say he *is* a body; it is correct to say he *has* one. The body is not he; he is more than it is.

And even as this man lives in the environment of a real and physical world, he lives also in an environment beyond this one. Being of spirit kind, he lives in a context of spiritual reality. His spiritual environs are no less real than his physical ones. As, by means of his body, he is in communication with the physical context in which he is, so, by some means, he needs to be in communication with the spiritual. It is not enough that, like the pig, he relate only to a material world of nipples and earth and roots and worms. If he is to be the whole man he is meant to be, if he is to live the whole life given him to live, then he must come alive not only to the physical surroundings which encompass him, but also to the spiritual as well.

He who has been born once stands in need of being born again. He who was born of the flesh needs to be born of the spirit. By birth, he came alive once to the physical world around him; by birth now once again he needs to come alive to another world, the spiritual.

It may be said, I believe, that it takes two births to produce a whole person. This was made clear by Jesus in his conversation with Nicodemus. No language could have made it plainer: "That which is born of the flesh is flesh, and that which is born of the Spirit is spirit." (John 3:6) The quality of spirit is there, present in every person, an essential of what a person is. But it is often dormant and inert until touched by some awakening spark which causes it to spring to life.

"You must be born anew," said Jesus to Nicodemus (John 3:7). Uncomprehendingly Nicodemus said, "How can a man be born when he is old?" (3:4) Jesus told him that the idea of another birth should not be something to marvel about. With Jesus, who knew better than anyone the spiritual character of our life, the prospect of coming alive spiritually was altogether as logical, as normal, as necessary, as the prospect of coming alive physically.

"Can a man enter a second time into his mother's womb and be born?" asked Nicodemus (3:4). Jesus quickly let him know that it was not this kind of birth of which he spoke.

Yes, of course, there is a measure of imagery here. Perhaps the word "birth" used in this way is actually a figure of speech — for physical terms are commonly used to portray spiritual reality. As a matter of fact, we really have no way to speak of purely spiritual phenomena except in physical terms. We must produce mind pictures which suggest or parallel spiritual truth if we are to communicate that truth at all. Jesus might possibly have said to Nicodemus, "You must undergo transformation from a state of spiritual unawareness to a condition of spiritual aliveness." But he didn't; he made it more dramatic, more specific, more vivid.

The birth of a human child into this world is exciting. So is the other birth about which we speak — exciting, thrilling, soul-stirring. The first birth, as everyone knows, is a new beginning; and so is the second one — a new start on a higher level and a scale more grand. If a physical birth is the start of a supreme adventure, as indeed it is, then a spiritual birth is the beginning of another adventure altogether as wonderful as the first one could ever be. After all, Jesus says that it is only in being born anew that we may see the Kingdom of God — and, understood rightly, there is never anywhere any higher adventure than that.

The late Dr. E. Stanley Jones vividly reminded us of the five kingdoms with which we have to relate. At the bottom, in the lowest position, is the mineral kingdom, the realm of inert things. Next up the scale is the vegetable kingdom, the realm of living things of plant kind. The stone by the roadside, could it speak, might say that no thing could put roots into the ground, spread leaves to the sun and grow; but the rosebush, if it knows anything, knows better. The rosebush, in turn, could it speak, might say that no thing could run about on legs and at will issue sounds from a throat; but your dog knows better, for he is of a realm higher than the vegetable, the animal kingdom. The dog might say, could he speak, that no kingdom could be higher, for after all no dog ever wrote a sonnet, sang an aria, painted a landscape, or built a cathedral. But man has done these things and more, and man knows, if he things, that he is of a kingdom higher than the mere animal, that they are of the human kingdom, the realm of humanity.

But is this all? Does the scale of being stop here? Does it end with man? No. There is God. And there is the KINGDOM OF GOD. It is clear beyond question that it is God's will to involve us of the human kingdom in his Kingdom — we are invited in, and

God has opened the gates of communication between the two. His higher Kingdom has already, in fact, entered into our lower one by incarnation. If we have had the spiritual sight with which to view him, we have seen already that higher Kingdom in the face and character of Jesus Christ. We will do well to listen as Jesus says, "It is your Father's good pleasure to give you the Kingdom." (Luke 12:32) He wants us to come alive to the sublime spiritual context in which (*anno Domini*) our lives are cast. Thus, with good reason, Jesus is saying: If you want to see the Kingdom, you must be born from above, come alive to the realm of spirit.

What does it mean to come alive to anything? It is of extreme importance that we understand this. It was Herbert Spencer, I believe, who first defined life as "the ability of an organism to respond to its environment." The definition is valid, and it offers considerable illumination of what we are talking about here.

What is the environment in which we humans have our being? Is it simply a perimeter of land and sea and sky? No, it is much more than this. Is it merely an assembly of material substance we can see and touch? No, it is infinitely more. To get some notion of what our environment really is, let us listen to something said by the Apostle Paul. At the Areopagus in Athens he gave vivid expression to a fundamental insight of the Christian faith — also, incidentally, a rather common tenet of Greek philosophy. Concerning God, Paul said, "IN HIM WE LIVE AND MOVE AND ARE." (Acts 17:28) Literally, we live in the environment of — God. And — it is of crucial importance to us that we be alive to the environment in which we do our living.

Please think with me now just a wee bit about ourselves and our environment. The stone by the roadside has no ability to respond to its environment. It cannot react to the rain that falls upon it, or the snow; it cannot make response to the shining sun or the thunder that rumbles across the sky on a stormy day. But, then, it isn't an organism. Yes, much of it was perhaps once organic — crustacean shells, bones of fish, reeds and rushes that once grew beside some primeval sea. But now it is thing only, inert, lifeless, non-responding.

Nearby a passing vehicle has struck a neighborhood house cat, leaving the mangled carcass, still warm from the pulse of life but lifeless now, lying at the roadside. The little creature no longer responds to a familiar voice saying, "Here, kitty," or to the smell of milk in its feeding dish. It is alive no longer to any of its environment, not even the roar of rushing traffic or the crunch of whirling wheels.

And then there is the pig in the field not far away. Very much alive he is at feeding time to the farmer's voice calling, "Piggy, piggy," and very much alive also to the itch that he tries to scratch away on the end of his feeding trough. But the sunset, orange and crimson in the west? No. He is not alive to that; it's just not a part of his world. The calla lilies that bloom in profusion just beyond the fence? No, he has never seen them, not really. The call of the whipporwill? No, he has never heard that, not really. He is, you see, alive to some things, dead to others. He lives in a limited world. This, of course, is because he is a pig, and such is the way of pigs, and, being a pig, he can be excused for being the way he is. Responding to the environmental elements which pigs' worlds are normally made of, this pig is in fact alive.

Now yonder in the huge white house on the hill is a man. Just now, in a silk dressing robe, he sits at a table on the flagstone veranda west of the house. A large man, he chews on a big, black cigar; on the table before him are three telephones, a decanter of alcohol, and many papers and ponderous ledgers he has brought here from one of his several offices. The sun is setting, but he doesn't see the sunset — hasn't seen it in twenty years. The roses are blooming in the garden, but the gardener takes care of them — this man doesn't know if they are there, and he doesn't care. Although the small son of his housekeeper has lain near death in a hospital for five weeks, he has not yet so much as inquired concerning the little fellow. His butler has instructions to hang up on anyone who telephones asking for anything.

Is this man alive? To some things, yes. He is alive indeed to dollar signs and ledgers, but he is not alive to very much else. He responds to certain segments of his environment, but there is no response to others. He lives in a limited world. Being a man, a person of humankind, he is not responding to the environmental elements which men's worlds are normally made of. He has, inherently, the ability to see the sunset, but he doesn't see it — for he is just not alive to the poetry-part of what is around him. Too bad, poor man; he is missing so much.

But let us suppose that this man — who can indeed do it — opens his eyes and heart to see the sunset, to appreciate the roses, to care about the child, to listen to the pleas of people in pain; let us suppose that he does become a more humane person. Will he then be complete, whole? Will he then be living in response to the full 360-degree circle of environment which surrounds him? Certainly he would be a much improved man, a more agreeable companion, easier to like. Surely he has come alive in areas where he was lifeless before, and now he is more alive than he was. Let us not forget, however, who he is: — He is man — and, being man, he is not fully alive until he is alive to God. The pig is a whole pig and fully alive when he can eat and sleep and awake to eat again, but not the man — his wholeness of life awaits an awareness of God and a living relationship with him.

The Christ says, "Behold, I stand at the door and knock." (Revelation 3:20) Will this man hear that knock? Will he open that door? The Christ says, "If any one hears my voice and opens the door, I will come in to him and will eat with him, and he with me." Will this man come alive to the presence of the One standing there? I hope he will, for the opened door through which Christ comes is the miracle opening by which a person comes alive to all that the Christ brings and means.

Holman Hunt did a painting which he entitled "The Light of the World." It depicts Jesus standing before a massive iron-bound wooden door. In the left hand he carries a lighted lantern, and his right hand is uplifted, knocking at the door. In an attitude of listening, there he stands waiting. On the surface of the door can be seen no latch or opening device of any kind. In one church a large wall-mounted reproduction of this picture had underneath it in bold lettering these words: "The latch is on the inside; only you can let him in." Seeing that picture, a small child said to his mother, "Why don't they let him in?" His mother answered, "I don't know, son, I don't know." After being thoughtfully silent for a while, the child said, "Mother, I think I know — they live in the basement, and they don't hear him knocking."

Tragically, it would appear, a good many people do indeed live in their basements. They seem never to get up to where it's bright and light and beautiful. Preoccupied with basement levels of living, they have never come alive to the presence of him who is always standing at life's front door.

You and I have been born into a real and physical world; by our very birth we have come alive to a whole complex of tangible circumstance (circumstance being "that which stands around" us). It makes its impingement upon us, and we know it. It touches us, and we feel the touch. It has many ways of getting our attention, of impressing itself upon us. If I put my hand into the fire, I am burned — the fire, without any hesitation at all, lets me know that it is there and that I'd better respect its presence and its power. If I step off the south rim of the Grand Canyon, thinking that I will walk on air to the north rim, the law of gravitation is there to shout at me, "You can't do that!" If I strike my finger with a hammer, this part of my body cries out in protest of pain. Abused or neglected, my stomach talks back to me. Around me and within my body itself, my physical circumstance compels me to be aware.

But the spiritual circumstance does not shout at me as the physical does. It may speak sometimes only in a whisper. But it is there. Being, as I am, man, I do my living in two environments, the physical and the spiritual. By my birth into this world, I have come alive to the one — heat and cold, sun and wind, and all the rest. By being born anew, of the Spirit, from above, I may come alive to the other — the wonder of God in Christ, the miracle of an all-encompassing love.

It's great to be alive! It's great to have been born into this world we share. It's great to see a mountain capped with snow, a wide expanse of ocean rolling high and strong, a white cloud flying against the blue, a wren's nest on the low limb of a backyard tree. It's great to hear the song the wind sings when it plays with autumn leaves, the sound of water running, the chirp of crickets, the hum of a bumble bee amid the clover blooms. It's great to feel the new grass of springtime beneath your feet, the stem of a rose between your fingers, the cool caress of a July breeze drifting in from the sea. Yes, it's great, isn't it, to be alive to this wonderful world into which, by birth, we have come? It's great to have the adventure of living!

But it's greater still to be alive to him whose own the snow-topped mountains are! The great adventure of living is greater still when all of earth's wonders are seen and heard and felt with perceptions amplified by being tuned in with the master Architect of them all.

If there is inspiration in the view of a distant star, the inspiration is greater yet when, in communion with the Lord of all stars, we can quietly and confidently talk with God in prayer. If it is good to enjoy this remarkable planet on which our birth has placed us, it is better yet to experience the world of spiritual relationship to which we have come alive by being born anew.

When All Things Are Yours

Second Sunday after Pentecost

"The Sabbath was made for man . . ." — Mark 2:27

As a teacher, Jesus did not work by appointment. He used the occasion, whatever it was, to make his points. He took advantage of opportunities which came along day by day as he walked and talked with his disciples and the multitudes. Many of his most extraordinary sayings were spoken in context of rather ordinary circumstance. In connection with quite limited and local situations, Jesus often spoke some far-reaching and universal word. Speaking to a few on one issue, he had a way of speaking to all humanity in all time on issues far more profound.

We have exactly this in Mark 2:23-28. Jesus was walking through the fields with his disciples on the sabbath day, and those inevitable nit-pickers, the Pharisees, were there. These men objected when Jesus' disciples plucked a little of the growing grain, shelled it in their hands, and ate it. Violation of the sabbath day! they screamed. Jesus didn't enter into an argument with them about this; he simply pointed them to an immense, overarching, transcending truth. "The sabbath was made for man, not man for the sabbath," he said.

You and I, my dear friends, need to understand the tremendous meaning for us of this thing which Jesus was saying to those Pharisees in that wheatfield long ago. It has to do with a lot more than how we act on Saturday, or Sunday, or any other day of the week. What is for whom — this is the issue.

It is quite clear that Jesus was saying we need the sabbath — and, because we need it, therefore we have it. God knows, as we should, that we need a time of worship and recovery. So Jesus was saying to the people of that ancient day: The sabbath is for you, it is in your interest; it is yours to help you, to serve you at your points of need. It does not stand as an overlord, commanding you; instead, it is rather like a friend who stands by on call to aid and assist you. The sabbath is among your ministers, ministering to you; you are not to serve it; it is to serve you. So, "The sabbath was made for man, not man for the sabbath.''

Nor is the sabbath the only thing that was made for man. The great "maker of things" has been most thoughtful of us in the way he has put his world together. And if you and I are tuned in with God, if we are walking with Christ, if we are lined up with life, if we are going with the grain of the universe, then we have an especially large retinue of servants who are ministering to us and helping us along. So much is ours! In fact, *if you belong to Christ, all things belong to you*! Maybe you know it, perhaps you do not, but, my dear Christian friend, you are rich — you have far more than the whole assembly of Rockefellers and Rothchilds and Vanderbilts all put together (if you think only of their material wealth).

Let me give you some background on an amazing verse from the Bible. Paul had been to Corinth, had spent considerable time ministering there. Later he wrote to the Corinthians, and in his letters one of the major concerns was the fact that these people were not getting along well with one another. They were fussing among themselves, feuding, fighting. The issue? Whom to follow. Some said Paul was the best preacher, some said Apollos (who also had been there), and some said Peter, or Cephas (who likewise had been one of their ministers). Each of these men had a following among the Corinthians, and these groups had become factions, at loggerheads with one another. One group was saying, "We belong to Paul"; another, "We belong to Apollos"; another, "We belong to Peter.''

In Paul's first letter (1 Corinthians 3:21-23) he writes this amazing thing: "Let no one boast of men. For *all things are yours*, whether Paul or Apollos or Cephas or the world or life or death or the present or the future, all are yours; and you are Christ's; and Christ is God's.'' Stop boasting of these various men, Paul says, stop your glorying in them; realize who these men are — realize what everything is — all of it belongs to you; it is your servant; you are not to serve it; it is to serve you. All of it belongs to you because you belong to Christ. Paul is saying: Because you belong to Christ, everything is helping you, ministering to you — everything, including the important men you debate about, and the world and life and death and the present and the future, it's all yours.

Paul's message here is startling, exciting: — Because you are rightly related to God through Christ, you are in right relationship with everything else — you are geared in, tuned in, on living terms with the universe, at peace with what is. Being Christian, you have come to terms with reality, lined up with ultimate truth, adjusted to the way things are made, set yourself in alignment with the way things are going to go at last. As you can hold a mirror in your hand, catch a ray of the mighty beaming sun and reflect it this way or that, so can you receive all the input of God's vast creation and let it serve you as your own.

In nature, the law of gravitation will pull down your house if you build it out of plumb, but that very law will help you if you build your house straight up and down. That law, which normally pulls things down, will be working for you if every brick is laid flat and square upon the one beneath it. But if your house leans, sooner or later the roof will fall in upon you.

Paul is saying that when life is brought into co-incidence with the way life is designed to work, everything is working for it. This is the meaning of Romans 8:28: "We know that in everything God works for good with those who love him . . . according to his purpose." To borrow an idiom from modern slang, being "groovy," the Christian is the most in-the-groove person anyone could ever imagine!

Yes, the sabbath is yours — and so are Paul, and Apollos, and Cephas, and the world, and life and death, and the present, and the future, and so on and on. Will you join me now in a little adventure of discovery? I think you'll be thrilled to discover what all of this really means to you.

The WORLD is yours! all its inspiration and fellowship. As a Christian, you have not walled yourself away from it behind some towering mountain of guilt. You are in communion with it; you are receptive to the messages spoken by stars and seas and mountains; you know the language of whispering wind and sunsets and rainbows. There is a mountainous difference between a criminal hiding himself in a dark alley and a person standing straight with lifted face on a hilltop under the arch of an October sky.

The world is yours! unobscured by dollar signs or gun-sights; the view is unmarred by bars of any cage of self-imprisonment whither you have run for refuge, undistorted by the warped prisms of prejudice through which others sometimes look. The world is not your master; in its presence you stand up tall and look it straight in the eye. You are in league with it, and in friendship with every lovely and worthy thing it offers.

But this isn't all: MEN are yours! (Yes, girls! do you hear?) Seriously, everyone, men are yours — Paul, Apollos, Cephas — and Beethoven, Michelangelo, Shakespeare, Lincoln. These and others of yesterday, and those of today with whom you walk and work, with whom you play and pray, between whose lives and yours there is an interflow of the stuff of which life is made. Your fellow-persons of our humankind, they are yours in fellowship, your ministers helping you, yours in *relationship* boosting you along.

From the great and good of the world past and present you receive inspiration, guidance, and strength. Your enemy, if you have one, is yours, too. A person cannot master you, cannot really hurt you, cannot really get to you. You love that person, as Jesus said you should. If someone hungers, you feed that person. One's hate, if one hates, cannot reach your heart — you are above that.

LIFE is yours. You do not deal with it as though you were wrestling some contrary thing. You are not scheming to squeeze from it some last drop of something you want. You are in league with life; you don't have to slip up on its blind side in the dark and snatch some morsel of happiness or comfort. You and life are on good terms, and across the years you can walk with it arm in arm, hand in hand.

Life cannot buffet you and beat you down. Trouble and afflictions? Yes, of course. But with the Apostle Paul you can say, "This slight momentary affliction is preparing for us an eternal weight of glory beyond all comparison." (2 Corinthians 4:17) Contrary winds may blow, but your sail is set to use them.

I once wondered how a wind-driven ship could be sailed against the wind. I had no problem understanding how it could be made to go the other way, with the wind. But how could the same wind which drove it in one direction be made to drive it in the other? Living for a while along the "stern and rockbound New England coast," I discovered this navigational feat is accomplished by "tacking," by a special setting of the sails. The sails are so adjusted that the ship zig-zags into the wind, a few degrees to starboard, then a few degrees to port, and back and forth, angling into the wind first this way and then that, so that the overall direction of movement is straight into the breast of the wind. As Ella Wheeler Wilcox so beautifully writes in one of her poems, it is "the set of the sail, and not the gale" which determines the way ships go. Likewise, as she points out, in our life it is the "set of the soul that decides the goal," and not the circumstances of the day.

So, dear friend of Christ, life is yours. Whatever the years may bring, you have learned how it is that sails are set. No, you cannot control the direction of the wind, but whatever direction it blows, it is yours, because you can use it as a power for going on.

And if life is yours, so is DEATH. For death is merely a part of life. If you belong to Christ, both life and death belong to you. Death is simply your conveyance from life this side of it to life beyond it. You are on a journey and death is your way of getting home. You are an "heir of God and a joint-heir with Christ."

(Romans 8:17) and death is your only way into the inheritance which awaits you yonder. The facts of life include the fact of death, and you have accepted this. When comes the time, you will use death as your means of reaching the rest of life. When that wind blows, your sail will be set to receive its thrust, and you'll go on. Death is not your enemy; it will not hurt you.

Have you read of John Chrysostom, that noble Christian saint of the fourth century? He was arrested by the Emperor of Constantinople and ordered to recant, to give up his faith in Christ. He refused, of course. There ensued then in the court an illuminating discussion as to what his punishment should be. When imprisonment was suggested, it was pointed out that Chrysostom would merely use the solitude for meditation and prayer in which he would rejoice. It was then suggested that he be flogged, whipped, made to suffer physically. To this suggestion it was said by some of the more enlightened of his accusers that as a follower of Christ he would count it an honor to undergo this kind of suffering as his Christ had. Banishment was recommended by some, and others argued that this would serve no useful purpose, since he would merely go about the world telling everywhere the story he loved to tell, the story of Jesus and the love of God. When it was at last proposed that he be put to death, everyone knew that he wouldn't mind dying because he believed steadfastly in a better world beyond.

Well, they killed Chrysostom at last, but they never hurt him. He belonged to Christ. He was committed to Christ, committed beyond injury. Death was his, you see; and death is yours also, my dear Christian friend.

On the evening of December 4, 1952, a worse-than-usual fog settled over the British city of London. At one subway exit hundreds of people, homebound from their work, poured out onto the darkened street. No one was able to see anything beyond the reach of his own arm. But a man was there to meet them, groping his own way confidently through the dark. Asking them their street addresses, unerringly he guided many to their homes. When asked how he could do it, the man replied, "I am blind; and to a blind man the fog makes no difference." He had grown up in that neighborhood, had lived there all his life, and he knew even all the potholes in the streets and the cracks in the sidewalks.

The power to see, which most consider essential, this man didn't need any more; he had gone beyond that. The darkness was his — not an enemy to be overcome; as a result of his sightlessness, he had overcome it already. The darkness could not master him; he was master of it. It wasn't in command, he was. He had suffered the loss of his sight, but he had gained mastery of the darkness.

Paul wrote in Philippians 3:8: "I have suffered the loss of all things . . . in order that I may gain Christ . . ." And having gained him, Paul had gained everything else. Death, my friend, is not your master — you belong to Christ, and he is in command. "I am alive . . . and I have the keys of Death . . ." he said (Revelation 1:18). And the keys he has are mightier than any chains that can ever bind you. Because you are his, death is yours, an instrument to reach that for which life is meant.

Nor is this all: The PRESENT is yours. Strange, perhaps, you think, that Paul should include this here, but he does, and truly it deserves an honored place on the roster of what is yours. Many persons have no present — today is not theirs at all. Some, for example, miss today waiting for tomorrow. Here is the student who is waiting until he can get out of school, who thinks life will start on graduation day. Here is the youth who believes life will begin when he can start driving the family car. Or here is the factory worker who idles along through the boring hours under the illusion that life will commence when he can get the foreman's job. All these, waiting for tomorrow, are missing today. And you can illustrate this in a thousand ways from now until this time next year. It is happening all the time: the present is sacrificed upon the altar of some vague tomorrow.

Others have no present for precisely the opposite reason: they are living, such life as they have, in the past. Wishing yesterday's good to come back, or resenting yesterday's bitter thing, they wander in down-spiraling circles along devious paths of memory. Locked in with what has been, they somehow miss the wonder of all that is.

But with you, Christian friend, it is not so. The present is yours because, as Paul said, you are Christ's. "I am alive forevermore . . ." he says; and this includes today. "I am with you always," he says; and this includes now. You don't have to go back to any past to find a life worth living — you don't have to wait for any future. It is true to say, "Christ lived." It is true to say, "Christ shall live." But it is also true to say, "He lives!" The living Lord is Lord of the living Present, and because you belong to him, you live also, and the present belongs to you.

And do not forget this, never let any circumstance come between you and this fact: the FUTURE is yours. You belong to One who is master of the endless years. You cannot know the mystery of what the future holds, but you can be sure of the mastery of him who holds it in his hands. The future cannot "lord it over you" with leering face or paralyze you with some foreboding fear. You belong to the Lord of unending tomorrows, and you don't have to be afraid. As a Christian, you have lost your life to find it again — on a higher level, in a cosmic fellowship. "You are not your own"; (1 Corinthians 6:19) you belong to the Lord of the long, long road. You have made peace with the tomorrows, whatever they bring. They cannot command you; they are yours. Embrace them heartily and they will serve you well.

So, my dear one, take note of what you have going for you! Be aware how rich you are! Recognize the legions of servants who stand by to help you along your way. Yes, of course, the sabbath day is yours — and so are all the other days — and so much more: the world and life and death and the present and the future. All of this is yours — because of whose you are.

Therefore, pilgrim friend, as you go forth into the supreme adventure of whatever lies ahead, if you are ever tempted to believe that all things are against you, remember to whom you belong and know that this cannot be so. However intense the storm, however dark the day, however dim the view, say sincerely in your heart, "Because I belong to Christ, everything belongs to me." Always remember that you belong to One to whom all things belong.

How to Test a Spirit

Third Sunday after Pentecost

"How can Satan cast out Satan . . . ?" — Mark 3:23

Having seen one of the world's master magicians do one of his baffling tricks, I turned to my wife and said, *"How* did he do that?" My question was the inevitable one. Almost without exception, when we see someone do something we cannot explain, we say, "How did he do it?" When someone makes a spectacular achievement, succeeds where others had failed, or performs that which we had assumed impossible, we want to know by what power or skill it was done. We do not tolerate mystery well; we want it all cleared up. Our nature is such that it is usually difficult for us to accept what we do not understand.

So it was with the Pharisees, scribes, and many others when Jesus was going about in Palestine saying and doing the uncommon things which were so common with him. In the third chapter of Mark we are told that Jesus healed many persons, restored the withered hand of one man, and generally confounded all witnesses by his remarkable works. The Pharisees, the Herodians, and the scribes held counsel concerning all of this. They just had to come up with some kind of explanation, preferably one that would incriminate and discredit Jesus.

After consultation, they made the announcement of their findings: "He is possessed by Beelzebub," they said (Mark 3:22). Now Beelzebub was considered to be a prince among demons, and they were saying that the amazing power of Jesus was an evil power. They saw illness as a result of demonic work in human persons, and they were saying that "by the prince of demons" Jesus was casting out demons.

This analysis Jesus rejected forthwith. Having confounded those people with his magnificent healing works, he now confounded them with a question: "How can Satan cast out Satan?" (Mark 3:23) Is Satan risen up against himself? he asked. Is evil working against its own purpose? Anyone knows that a kingdom or a house divided against itself is soon coming to an end.

There is no record that the Pharisees had any further argument to offer.

You see, they had made a mistake; they had misjudged Jesus. Out of his loving and compassionate heart, with a kind and compassionate spirit, Jesus had done some helpful things for some folks. But his enemies were crediting his good works to a different kind of spirit. They were saying it was an evil spirit which prompted him and empowered him. So anxious were they to explain what they had seen and to bring Jesus into disrepute that they grossly misconceived the spirit which moved him.

It seems to me that you and I can learn a useful and needful lesson at this point. Here we can gain an insight by which we will be immensely helped in our daily living. One thing, it seems to me, we urgently need to know and never forget is that *all of us are spirit-possessed.* And one art, I am sure, we need to try to master is the fine art of testing and measuring the spirits within ourselves and in others. Let us put our minds together now to think about this a little.

Please do not be shocked when I say that all of us are spirit-possessed. Let me tell you what I mean, and you can understand the truth of this. To illustrate, let us consider an event in the ministry of Paul which is related for us in the sixteenth chapter of the Acts of the Apostles.

There was a certain "slave girl who had a spirit of divination and brought her owners much gain by soothsaying." (16:16) It appeared to many that this girl was able to know things and do things which others could not. She was something of a curiosity, and her owners made a kind of "side show" of her, getting money for themselves. This poor, demented creature, abused and used, this wild thing, driven — there has been a lot said about her and about this sort of thing, about what it means to be possessed by a spirit.

It seems to me, however, that there were some other people in this story who also were spirit-possessed. There were the girl's owners, who apparently had no "spirit of divination," but certainly they were moved by a spirit of selfish greed, unfeelingly and cruelly using her, preying on her sickness. And there were the rulers, the magistrates, and some of the citizens of Philippi who, although not afflicted with "a spirit of divination," were certainly possessed by spirits of narrow bigotry, more concerned with *status quo* than with truth.

Then, too, in this same chapter of Acts we meet Lydia of Thyatira. There is no evidence that she had any spectacular spiritual powers, but, bless her heart, this good woman was surely possessed by a spirit of helpfulness and devotion and kindness and generosity, making her name a synonym for gentle womanhood to this very day.

How frequently we hear it said concerning some person that "she has a sweet spirit," or that "he has a bitter spirit," or that one has a "generous spirit," or another a "selfish spirit." These are common expressions which we hear and use almost daily. We commonly recognize, you see, that within us are those "spirits" whose presence is made known by what we say and do — and sometimes by the ways in which we say what we say and do what we do, the spirit in which we go about the overt aspects of our living.

Some may say it's not a matter of spirit, but of attitude. Perhaps. Attitude, however, suggests merely a posture of mind, and anyone who knows life very well knows that life goes deeper than mind goes, and that actions often spring from levels much deeper than intellect. By whatever name called, there are powerful moving forces deep within us, and we are pretty much on target when we call them spirits — whether sweet or bitter, generous or selfish.

Well, now, these spirits within us — how do they get there? where do they come from? We may say that they invade us from outside, and there is a certain truth in this. There are indeed strange, mysterious, super-material forces at work in our world. Paul recognizes this in Ephesians 6: "We are not contending against flesh and blood, but . . . against the world rulers of this present darkness, against . . . spiritual hosts of wickedness . . ." We read in our Bible of "the spirit of the world" and "the Spirit which is from God." (1 Corinthians 2:12) We read of "the spirit of truth and the spirit of error." (1 John 4:6) Paul was stating an important truth when he wrote: "Do you not know that to whom you yield yourselves servants to obey, his servants you are whom you obey?" (Romans 6:16) Thinking of a world struggle for possession of the human heart, someone has written:

> The soul of man, Jehovah's breath,
> That keeps two worlds at strife —
> Hell moves to work its death
> And heaven stoops to give it life.

But to say all of this is to state only a partial truth. The picture of the human person as a prize or pawn in a battle being waged outside himself is a picture not altogether accurate. There is also a battle within. Not all spirits originate in some other world and invade ours; the spirits that possess us do not always come into us from somewhere outside, but grow up and develop within. The spirits which move us are many times very much our own. They are pretty largely our own doing; they are what we have nurtured and cultivated, what we have made of the basic stuff of our human nature-hood. I strongly suspect that most spirits with which we have to do are not nebulous, slithering shapes of ectoplasm, but are quite human phenomena, bright or dark, good or ill, which arise within us and grow until, to this extent or that, they take possession of us.

And these spirits, in whatever manner they assume their control of us, are very assertive. They are not idle, they do not hibernate. They rise up to color or control our actions, to manage our lives and boss us around in more ways than we sometimes care to admit. We have them, possess them as ours, until, at length, they possess us. Every once in a while when some fellow does some outlandishly stupid thing, someone is heard to say, "What possessed him?" The question is a common and natural way of saying, "I wonder what made him do that." The phrasing of the question, not carefully thought out but rather instinctive, is probably quite appropriate.

Around us and within us, ours is a world filled with forces which seek to capture and control us at the mental and spiritual levels of our being. All about us are the cross-currents of blowing winds, and some people unfurl their sails to this wind and some to that one. We are unceasingly making choices among the many influences which knock at our doors seeking admission to the inner depths of what we are.

So we do need to monitor diligently the spiritual happenings within us. Whatever the origin of the spirit may be, whether it is one which approaches from without or arises from within, we need to be on guard. And this brings us to the second important consideration in this matter: that is, the fine art of testing spirits. The Pharisees around Jesus did a pathetically poor job of this.

I believe, if we try a little, we can learn to do better, and it's of extreme importance that we do. How unfair it is, and sometimes how painful or tragic, when we misread the spirit of another person. And it is, of course, a dangerous error when we wrongly identify the spirits which move within ourselves.

1 John 4:1 is both a fascinating thought and a bit of extremely good advice: "Do not believe every spirit, but test the spirits to see whether they are of God." Why should this be necessary? The writer says, "because many false prophets (or spokesmen) have gone out into the world." Not every voice is a valid voice; not all voices are equally reliable. In 1 Corinthians 14:10 Paul writes: "There are so many kinds of voices in the world . . ." Revelation

16:14 speaks of "devil spirits, performing signs . . ." At Babel there may have been a "confusion of tongues," but everywhere that we of humankind live and feel and move, there is a troublesome confusion of spirits.

Knowing this, God moves into the scene saying, "I will pour out *my* Spirit upon all flesh . . ." (Joel 2:28) At Pentecost the Apostle Peter declared that on that day this promise of God had been fulfilled. (Acts 2:16) Whatever spirits of good or evil are rattling the doorlatches of our lives, we may be sure that the Spirit of God is there. Among all the confusion, he wants us to identify his Spirit and let him take possession.

So the word of John is a highly important one to every one of us: "Do not believe every spirit, but test the spirits to see whether they are of God." A soldier on sentinel duty, peering cautiously into the darkness, listens for the sound of anything moving there. Hearing only the slightest of sounds, he readies his rifle and shouts his challenge: "Who goes there?"

In much the same way, we need to post sentinels on all perimeters of our lives. Old Edinburgh Castle, standing strong in Scotland on Castle Rock, was unconquerable for many years. There was, however, on one side a precipice so abrupt and so high that it was believed unscalable, and so was left without defense. To this point the enemy came; here he scaled the cliffs and breached the wall, and thus was the castle conquered — from its only unguarded side. On our life's every point of exposure, we need to be sure our sentinels are on the alert. And, likewise, we need to be on guard within our gates, alert to detect the uprising of any spirit unworthy of what we are.

Well, how do we do it? How do you test a spirit? I doubt if there is an easy formula that will fit all persons and all circumstances. But there are some things that may be said about it. So let us note some of these which can be briefly said.

First, I think I will be suspicious of any spirit which comes to me and demands haste. If the spirit which wants to move me is unwilling to stand the test of at least a little passing time, I will be cautious of it. It is time which at length will put all things in perspective, and whatever is afraid of the light of time I will suspect of having something to hide. Often when in anger or under stress one is about to do the precipitious thing, some very good friend will say, "You'd better stop and count to ten." There is good reason for this.

I know there are times when we must act, when we must move, when to delay would be to lose momentum or to invite disaster. But the fact is that very often a "haste spirit" seeks to avoid the proof of time, the light of truth. The "haste spirit" operates somewhat in the manner of a con artist, a kind of "slicker" who slips up to you surreptitiously, winks at you knowingly, and then, while he furtively looks both ways, whispers in your ear, "Now, right now, before someone else catches on to this, before someone gets wise to it, before someone interferes and spoils it, let me do you a big favor, let me let you in on something really good." Time is on the side of right, and wisdom, and truth. And the spirit which says, "Hurry up — don't wait," is one which I will want to examine critically and with care.

Second, I will be suspicious of the spirit which offers ease, which argues that this road or that one is the best road to take because it's the easiest road to some distant place. In our world the higher purposes usually call for work, effort, dedication, perhaps some measure of sacrifice. The pursuit of the great ideal leads often along the lonely trail; only the up-hill roads ever reach the summits. The easy roads are the down-grades, and "easy street" is usually a dead end. When we drift with the currents we are always going down. We live in a world where weeds will grow without any help from us, but where vegetable gardens and flowers require a lot of labor on our part. Evil in our world can maintain itself very well, thank you — but that which is good requires unceasing struggle.

Yes, I know there are sometimes easier paths which are good ones, and thank God for them. But these paths are usually the late ones, coming after the long climb. Character and goodness on the one hand and evil and ugliness on the other, both cost. For character and goodness we pay mostly in advance with discipline, self-control, labor, and struggle. For evil and ugliness we pay mostly afterward with bitterness, remorse, and regret. Someone has quaintly said, "The devil offers his best first, and God gives his best at the end." If there are some easy roads out yonder somewhere on life's sunlit plateaus, we must not forget that there are first on this side of them some rugged trails that call for muscle-strain and sweat. So, if any spirit comes to me and says, "Here, take the easy way," I think I will answer, "Where to?"

In the third place, I will try hard to reject the spirit which appeals to my weakness — the spirit which appeals to my fears when I ought to venture, to my selfishness when I ought to give, to my laziness when I ought to work. I will try hard to be open to the spirits that, instead of strengthening my weaknesses, help to make me strong against them. And I think I must be wary of whatever spirit asks me to jeopardize tomorrow's happiness in the interest of today's pleasure.

Then, also, I will try to mount a massive resistance against any spirit which excuses me from being my best or doing my most. The spirit of "get by" is one which wants to rob me of life's finest ventures. The spirit which says, "This is good enough," is trying to freeze me in my tracks, to stop me where I am. Someone has truthfully said, "The worst enemy of the best things in life are the merely good things." I don't think Michelangelo became Michelangelo by splashing some paint at a canvas and saying, "That's good enough."

It is a pathetic non-realization of life to be content with minimums when the maximums are out there waiting. A good story is told of a boy walking along the street, whistling in a tuneless sort of way. A man, hearing, said, "Son, can you whistle a tune?" Replying, "Yes, sir," the boy then proceeded to whistle beautifully. When the tune was finished the man said, "Son, if you can whistle like that, whatever made you whistle the other way in the first place?" This is a good question: concerning whistling or living.

There are many kinds of spirits in the world, around us and within. Some are our friends, seeking to guide us up to the higher levels and greater joys of living. Some, deceptive and deceitful, pose as our friends when in fact they are not. Paul wrote to Timothy the warning that "some will depart from the faith, giving heed to seducing spirits." (1 Timothy 4:1) Like Bunyan's Christian on pilgrimage to the heavenly city, on our journey we will encounter a motley variety of spirits who will try to draw us aside from the way. We must be vigilant, as John urged, to "test the spirits to see whether they are of God."

I have suggested some ways to do this; but the most reliable way I want to mention now. Through all this confusion of spirits there is One Spirit of unique and singular character, One Spirit spelled with a capital "S," One Spirit who is truly personal, for whom the common noun "spirit" becomes the proper noun, *his name*. For, as John tells us, God "has given us of his own Spirit." (1 John 4:13) Paul speaks of "The Holy Spirit . . . poured upon us richly through Jesus Christ . . ." (Titus 3:6) Peter writes of "The Holy Spirit sent from heaven . . ." (1 Peter 1:12) To Timothy the Apostle Paul writes of "The Holy Spirit who dwells within us . . ." (2 Timothy 1:14) The message is this: The Spirit of God is come, the Holy Spirit is with us.

And what is it he can do to help us? What is the role of the Holy Spirit in our lives? The answer is given in a very practical way by our Lord himself in John 14:26. Announcing the Spirit's coming, Jesus said, "The Holy Spirit, whom the Father will send in my name, he will teach you all things, and bring to your remembrance all that I have said to you.''

So, having the Holy Spirit with us, we can test any spirit by the very wisdom and insight of the Christ himself — for by the present ministrations of the Spirit, the ancient word of our Lord becomes the living word, concurrent with any moment of our experience. And what better way to test a spirit than by the wisdom and spirit of Christ? What better way to test a diamond than to view it alongside a stone that is known to be perfect and pure? The ultimate test of any spirit is to view it alongside that Spirit which is Holy. Here we have the touchstone of all our testing. In Christ and by his Spirit, God is with us in the necessity of our daily testing of the many spirits which seek to possess us and to manage and move us this way or that.

God's Transforming Alternative

Fourth Sunday after Pentecost

"A seed, when it is sown, grows . . ." — *Mark 4:32*

"A seed, when it is sown, grows . . ." This is being said by Jesus in Mark 4:32. He says this is what the Kingdom of God is like — a seed sown and growing.

The seed is small, but it produces a large plant. The mustard seed, of which Jesus here speaks, he says is "the smallest of all seeds," but the mustard tree which grows from it is "one of the greatest of herbs." To portray the Kingdom of God as a tiny seed becoming a mighty tree is to suggest immense change. And we could talk about this as an important aspect of this text, for truly the Kingdom of God does indeed involve vast dimensions of change, miracle proportions of transformation, both in ourselves and in our world.

Also, it is notable that the growth of the seed is slow. The seed does not instantaneously become what it will eventually be. Time must pass; the elements must do their thing; the process must run at its own pace to its appointed end. To portray the Kingdom of God as a slow — but certain — evolvement of the full-grown and fruitful plant is to suggest an ordered sequence of unfolding developments, each one awaiting the consummation of all former ones. And we could talk about this important aspect of this text, for surely the Kingdom of God does require the patience of long waiting and the faith that at last all things will be as they should.

But there is an insight here of even greater importance than either of these. To perceive it, let us think a little of what is happening as the seed becomes the tree.

Here it is — the tiny, almost microscopic thing, inert, a lusterless shade of brown, its visible features offering no sign of life. Around it is the brown earth, barren, made of what once was mountain stone and once-living things now long dead. Under it is the cool damp, the damp that rots things — the leaves that fall, the twigs, the logs, and most objects left unattended lying there. Above it is the hot sun whose beams, falling unimpeded, can burn like a fire. A person, unaccustomed to it and unprotected by clothing from it, will be actually burned to the death with a few days of uninterrupted exposure to it.

So here lies the seed, so apparently powerless, in its apparently hostile circumstance, seemingly a victim and doomed to decay. But it does not rot, and it does not burn up — it grows! And observe how it does.

First, something moves within it, or is moved. The moisture which rots other things penetrates its thin, brown shell. But decay does not start; something else does — there is a movement of something called life. It is nurtured by the very wetness which has already destroyed last year's bean stalk.

Then it bursts open, cracking its pod by a mysteriously mighty thrust from within, and a pale, fragile shoot peeps out into the cool, damp soil. But the warmth of the sun is tugging at it, and the shoot turns upward. It begins to reach, feeling its way, probing the clods, making a path for growing.

That frail shoot in a little while pushes aside the final clods, rends the surface with a crack, and breaks out into the light. Then, still reaching up, it unfolds delicate leaves and spreads them to the sun. And so it grows, this tiny seed, until there stands a tree, tall and strong.

Now suppose you were seeing a seed for the first time; suppose you had no prior knowledge at all of growing things. You hold it in your hand, this seed — an almost invisible and apparently worthless little thing, and you drop it carelessly into the ground, where all worthless and unwanted things tend to go. Then you see it change, this seed — you see it open, its shoot emerge, its leaves spread, and its limbs expand until it towers high above your head. A miracle! you would shout; a miracle has happened, you would say. Nor would you be far from right.

Well, here is the question: Why does not the seed decay? Why does it grow? Why does it not yield to the forces of deterioration around it? How can it convert these unfriendly elements into resources for its own transformation into something infinitely greater? The tiny thing would appear to be doomed to be always the tiny thing it is or to suffer the devastation of all decaying things. But it does not. And why? Because, implanted in the seed, built into its very nature, is AN ALTERNATIVE — an alternative to decay, an alternative to its doom. An *added ingredient* is there, an element we call life. And that element, this alternative, is mighty enough to overcome all the impinging powers of destruction and to make of itself a nobler thing.

What is Jesus saying to us in Mark 4:32? I think he is saying that God has put into the world *his glorious alternative*, and that this alternative is mighty enough to overcome every obstacle and to bring our life into what it is meant to be.

Now, will you let your mind range high and wide and think — on a grand scale — about God's glorious alternative, what it is and how it works. It is from our Bible, of course, that we learn more about this than we can expect to learn anywhere else — unless perchance it may be in the school of our own experience. So let us have a look at some things the Bible is saying to us concerning the transforming alternative which is present and working in our human affairs.

In language there are certain "turn-around" words. One such word is "but." We say, "It is a cold day, *but* we have a fire and therefore we are warm." Another of the "turn-around" words is "nevertheless." We say, "It is raining; nevertheless, because we have our umbrellas, we are not wet."

The word "and" is a "going-on" word. This word signals the addition of something of like kind, suggests continued momentum, further movement in the same direction. We say: There is this, *and* that, *and* the other. But "nevertheless" is a "turn-around" signal in that it points in a different direction, *introduces an alternative*, something on the other side.

We live, you and I, as human beings, in a malaise of difficulty and problem. The human scene is not all sunshine; it is crisscrossed with drifting shadows, buffeted by raging storms. Often in the human experience there is trouble and heartache, there are sorrows and pains — and there are sins and their consequences. All of this is here present; it seems to be an aspect of the way things are. It appears to be an element in the human equation, an integral component of life's "given."

In mathematics — geometry, for instance — we deal with the "given." The "given" is the fact which is there to start with: for example, a straight line is the shortest distance between two points. Well, in our human family it is quite apparent that we must also reckon with a "given." We cannot ignore it any more than we can ignore the axioms of plane geometry. It is there; it seems to be what we have to start with and cannot avoid. With its horrifying manifestations of depravity and conflict, brutality and "man's inhumanity to man," it would seem that we are as doomed to decay as a scrap of writing paper dropped on the ground and left to the mercy of the elements. So it would seem.

But . . . However . . . Nevertheless. Here we must use a "turn-around" word. There is something else in this picture. There is another side to be reckoned with. As within the seed there is an alternative to decay and death, so is there an alternative present in the kaleidoscopic complex of our human scene. God has put it there. Over against life's "given," he has provided a "given" of his own. Our humanity seems to be caught in a maelstrom from which we cannot get ourselves loose. But . . .

GOD GIVES. God gives HIS SON. God adds something, puts an additional element into the equation, tips the balance another way. Interjecting his love, he comes with a divine incursion into our human wilderness. Read it: "God so loved the world that he gave his only Son, that whosoever believes in him should not perish, but have eternal life." (John 3:16) A needed insight, often overlooked, is here, clearly said: "should not perish, BUT have eternal life." The perishing is there, it is on the way to happening, it is already in the works; this is the way the momentum is moving. BUT here comes the alternative, here in Jesus Christ is the countermanding power, the "turn-around" authority.

There is much in our New Testament which pictures humankind as in rebellion against God and the good and the light, as not in obedience to the rule and will and love of the heavenly Father. "BUT we see Jesus . . ." So it is written in Hebrews 2:9. He appears on the scene. He comes, bringing an offered alternative to our futility, folly, frustration, failure — and death.

In Paul's letter to the Ephesians, second chapter, the Apostle speaks of "the course of this world" (verse 2) as a course that is running tragically downgrade. He says (verse 3) that "among these" who walk this course "we all once lived in the passions of our flesh, following the desires of body and mind, and so were by nature children of wrath, like the rest of mankind." His is a picture of callous wrongfulness, of being "dead in trespasses and sins." Thank God, though, he doesn't stop with that picture, he doesn't leave us doomed to go in that direction. There comes the "turn-around" word (verses 4-6): "BUT God who is rich in mercy, out of the great love with which he loved us, even when we were dead through our trespasses, made us alive together with Christ . . . and raised us up with him . . ." You see, God crosses "the course of this world" with his redeeming alternative, opens up the possiblity of another direction.

However dismal our prospects may be, God comes in with his glorious "nevertheless." We may be all bound up in our sins, but God offers the "nevertheless" of sins forgiven. We read (Romans 6:23) that "the wages of sin is death, BUT the free gift of God is eternal life in Jesus Christ our Lord." We read (Proverbs 13:15, ASV) that "the way of transgressors is hard," and so it is — at last. But there is another way, an alternate way, "The new and living way which he opened for us" (Hebrews 10:20).

We may be all entangled with our troubles, but God offers the "nevertheless" of troubles transformed. Jesus said (John 16:20, 22): "You will be sorrowful, but your sorrow will turn into joy . . . You have sorrow now, but I will see you again and your hearts will rejoice." Such is the transforming power of God's "nevertheless" that we can know, however dismal the hour may be, "that this slight momentary affliction is preparing for us an eternal weight of glory beyond all comparison." (2 Corinthians 4:17) Much of what befalls us "at the moment" may seem "painful rather than pleasant; *but later* it yields the peaceable fruit of righteousness." (Hebrews 12:11) God's alternative is in there working, and, like the spark of life within a seed, in course of time it will produce the "peaceable fruit," the beautiful thing. Just wait. This is the key: "But later . . ." The divine "nevertheless" is working; believe, and let it work.

Our world may be all shrouded over with oppressive gloom, but God offers the "nevertheless" of a mighty, uplifting hope. In the second epistle of Peter we have a devastating picture of humanity at the very worst, persons who act "like irrational animals . . . blots and blemishes, reveling in their dissipation, carousing . . . having eyes full of adultery, insatiable for sin . . . slaves of corruption . . ." These people are portrayed as ungrateful, unbelieving, and immoral. Then Peter says, "*Nevertheless* (in spite of all this, regardless of the way things are), nevertheless, we . . . look for new heavens and a new earth wherein righteousness dwells." (2 Peter 3:13)

In the second epistle of Paul to Timothy we are given the picture of a world filled with depressing uncertainty and unfaithfulness, with apprehension and anxiety. Then Paul says, "Nevertheless, God's firm foundation stands." (2 Timothy 2:19)

You see, dear friend, that even as in nature God has put his glorious "nevertheless" into a tiny mustard seed, so into the realm of the human life-story he has put a "nevertheless" infinitely more glorious than any process of nature could ever be. Please do not think of all this as merely academic. Never! It is life. Nothing could ever be more real or more personal for you and me. It is not my wish to oversimplify history, but look with me quickly, if you will, at two or three episodes of our past.

Nebuchadnezzar, the king of Babylon, sent three Hebrew men into the fiery furnace, expecting that they would be quickly burned to the death by the flames, but somehow God moved in with his glorious "nevertheless," and when the king later looked into the flames he saw the three standing alive in the fire, and with them "the form of the fourth" who appeared "like a son of the gods." Darius, the king of Persia, tossed Daniel into a den of lions, expecting his body to be torn limb from limb and his flesh eaten by the hungry beasts. But in some way I suspect neither you nor I understand, God moved in with his glorious "nevertheless," and the mouths of the lions were shut. For 400 years, almost, the Egyptian Pharaohs held the Hebrew people as slaves in captivity, but God moved in with his glorious "nevertheless" and a man named Moses.

But please understand this: the mighty alternatives of God have not been in evidence in ancient history only — some are nearer our own time, and some are in it. God's "nevertheless" continues to be at work in our world. Let me tell you a story.

Adoniram Judson, pioneer missionary from America to Burma, has been called the father of American Christian missions. He was the oldest son of a Congregatonal minister in Massachusetts. A brilliant child, he was able to read by the age of three. At age nineteen he was graduated from Brown University, first in his class. But while a student there he came under the influence of a college buddy who was a militant opponent of Christianity. As a result of this influence, young Judson became an infidel, utterly rejecting his family's faith.

Sometime after his graduation from the university, unbelief and resentment rankling within him, he headed west, as he supposed, to achieve success and make a fortune. Late one evening he stopped at the hotel in a small town, seeking a room for the night. No room was available except one, and this one was next to a room where a young man was critically ill and dying. "It's pretty bad," said the hotel clerk. But Judson took the room. Through most of the night he heard the awful sounds that came from the room next door — ravings, cursings, and blasphemies unlike anything he had ever heard before.

Toward morning the young man died. A little later at the hotel desk Judson asked the name of that young man, and when the name was given he identified it instantly as that of his college chum. If this is the way it is to be an infidel, he said to himself, then I don't want to be one; if this is where it leads, then I want to travel a different road. That morning he headed his horse back to Plymouth and to his father's house. You see, the "nevertheless" of God was working in that midwestern hotel that night. Tragically, a young man was dying, but in a miracle sort of way, another young man was there to learn a lesson from that death, and his own life was turned around.

I have stood at a place on Court Street in Boston where a store clerk doing the routine work of selling shoes came one day into face-to-face encounter with God's glorious "nevertheless." There, on a wall alongside the entrance to Patton's Restaurant (as it was then, and perhaps still is), I read from a bronze plaque this inscription: "D. L. Moody, Christian Evangelist, Friend of Man, Founder of the Northfield Schools, was converted to God in a shoe store on this site, April 21, 1855." But for the intervention of God's glorious "nevertheless," the world would never have heard of Dwight L. Moody, but God did indeed move in with his magnificent redeeming alternative, and the world was blessed and moved mightily toward the good because of this man.

And if you will look thoughtfully about you, my friend, you will observe many another whose life course has been turned around — from the dark to the light, from wandering into wonder, from vascillation into venture — because a path has been crossed by the transforming "nevertheless" of God.

For my own part, I am humbly grateful for it, rejoice greatly in it, for I owe everything to it. If you will permit me to share my witness, I can tell you that I was among the rebels, a philosophical atheist, believing in no god and ridiculing the Christian's Bible. Then, presently, I was disillusioned and bitter, withdrawn, lonely, and desperate. But somehow God got to me with his life-changing "nevertheless," and I saw life as I had never seen it before. "I doubt it" had been my motto, but that was erased and I wrote in its place, "I believe." A bit of simple verse became meaningful to me, and it still is. Who wrote it I suspect nobody knows, but surely the author was spiritual kin of mine who felt and wrote these lines:

> *I questioned earth and heaven;*
> *I inquired of the day and night;*
> *I climbed to the heights of knowledge*
> *And traversed the fields of light.*
> *And I heard the world's loud voices*
> *Like the surge of a troubled sea,*
> *For the heart of man is restless*
> *Until it rests, O Lord, in thee.*

> *I go on my way victorious;*
> *I am done with the pain and strife;*
> *I drink of the mighty river*
> *That flows from the wells of life.*
> *And I hear the silent voices,*
> *Like the swell of the sleeping sea,*
> *For my heart, O Lord, rejoices —*
> *It has found its rest in thee.*

Well, my dear friend, on this journey we make together, whatever life brings to you, whatever the years do, whatever happens, whatever comes, whatever presses in upon you, restrains you, holds you — remember this: There is always the mighty redeeming alternative of God's glorious "nevertheless." If you look to the left and find it dark there, or to the right and see only the dim mists of uncertainty, then in Christ's name, *look up* — for God is offering *his own alternative* to *everything else*.

Conquering
the Grasshopper Complex

Fifth Sunday after Pentecost

"Why are you afraid . . .?" — Mark 4:40

The Sea of Galilee is actually a small freshwater lake about thirteen miles long and seven and a half miles wide. We usually think of it as a mountain lake, but its surface is really 682 feet below sea level, and the Jordan River, outflowing from it, runs its entire course below the level of the oceans.

Occasionally we read somewhere the story of some "drama on the high seas," and the story is usually one of a shipwreck or a rescue or some similar action-packed adventure. The Sea of Galilee can scarcely qualify as one of the "high seas," but much high drama has been played out on the blue-green waters of this historic lake. We may read of one of these in the fourth chapter of the Gospel according to Mark.

The actors in this drama were Jesus and several of his disciples. They were together in a boat going across to the opposite side of the lake, and we are told that "a great storm of wind arose," as indeed such storms often do in that remarkable place. The day had been an exhausting one, and Jesus was asleep in the boat. In the midst of the storm the disciples awakened him, saying, "Do you not care if we perish?" We are told that then Jesus rebuked the wind and said to the sea, "Peace! Be still!" The word is that the wind ceased and there was a calm across the sea.

We read the story and marvel. But the important thing is what happened next, as Jesus said immediately to his disciples, "Why are you afraid? Have you no faith?" When the harrowing episode was over and the storm had been stilled, Jesus did *not* say, "Fellows, did you take note of the way I stopped that wind and made those waves quiet down?" Instead, he asked them this question: "Why are you afraid?"

Now, of course, I do not know any better than you what Jesus had in mind when he asked his question. Perhaps he was concerned about their fear of the storm itself, their fear of drowning, of losing their lives. Perhaps he was concerned about some fear they may have had about what would happen to them after they drowned, if they did. Or maybe he was concerned about some fear they had of him, for it is said that they were "filled with awe" and said one to another, "Who is this, that even wind and sea obey him?"

But there is a second part to Jesus' question. The whole question: "Why are you afraid: have you no faith?" The question appears to make faith an alternative to fear: If you only had faith, there would be no cause, no occasion, for you to be afraid.

Perhaps Jesus' question implies that his disciples should have believed that they would survive the storm, that they would not perish as they thought they were about to, that between God's good care and their own skills of seamanship, they would come out of it all right. Or perhaps his question implies, more deeply, that his disciples should have trusted implicitly that even if they did not survive the storm, even if they drowned, everything would still be all right, that for the people of God drowning does not terminate life anyway. Or maybe his question implies, more deeply yet, that his disciples should have had the faith to believe that his own awesome power was being used, and always would be, not to frighten or awe them, but to help them and in their behalf. Or it could be that all three of these dimensions of faith were in the thought of Jesus when he asked his question.

Why are you afraid? The question could suitably be asked of many persons, for many are afraid — of this or that, of something or other. The story is told of a professional bill collector who worked on the theory that everyone is afraid of something. When asked why he was so successful in collecting debts on which all others had failed, he replied, "It's simple; I just write the delinquent people a letter telling them if they don't pay up at once that thing which they are afraid will happen will happen, and they always pay!"

I somehow doubt if fear is so utterly universal among us, but I am quite sure there is a lot of it around. And I am persuaded that much of the fear in the hearts of people is there because faith is not. In one way or another, a failure of faith has opened the way for fear to take over, the absence of faith having left a large vacancy into which fear can move.

The problem is not always a matter of lacking faith in *God*, although the lack of this is always a major forfeiture of life's high privilege. Sometimes the problem is a devastating lack of faith, or confidence, in *ourselves*. And sometimes the problem is a somewhat selfish or cynical lack of faith in *other persons*. But whatever default of faith there may be, it always has — to some extent and sometimes to great extent — a paralyzing effect upon us, afflicting us with a paralysis of fear.

We will be much helped here, I believe, if we will turn back and look at something which happened almost three and a half millenniums ago. The Israelites had gotten themselves free of Egypt and, on their journey to "the promised land," had reached the southern border of Canaan. During the nearly four centuries of their Egyptian exile, other peoples had migrated into their land and were well established up and down the Jordan valley and on the mountains and plains westward to the Mediterranean.

From Kadesh-barnea Moses sent spies into the land to search it out and determine the strength of the occupants. The spies were twelve in number, one from each of the twelve "tribes" of Israel. Moses said to the spies, "See what the land is, and whether the people who dwell in it are strong or weak, whether they are few or many, and whether the land that they dwell in is good or bad, and whether the cities they dwell in are camps or strongholds . . ." (Numbers 13:18-19)

In course of time the twelve men returned from their scouting trip and made their report to Moses and the people. All twelve of the spies agreed that the land was rich, "flowing with milk and honey." They agreed also that the people who dwelt in the land were strong, and that the cities were fortified and very large. They were unanimous in their findings that the land was highly desirable but strongly defended.

When it came, however, to the recommendation for action, there was a difference of opinion among them. Caleb, representing the tribe of Judah, and Joshua, of the tribe of Ephriam, said, "Let us go up at once and occupy the land, for we are well able to overcome it." The other ten disagreed, saying, "We are not able to go up against these people; for they are stronger than we." They reported that they had seen the Nephilim, the "sons of Anak," who were "men of great stature," giants. And then said these ten spies, "We seemed to ourselves like grasshoppers, and so we seemed to them." (Numbers, chapter 13).

As is common in such cases, the voice of the majority prevailed, and all that night the people wept, many making a clamor to return to Egypt and be slaves again — rather than go forward and fight against the "giants." They did not, of course, go back to Egypt, but the whole congregation of the people did turn south from there into the wilderness where for about forty years they wandered as nomads in the wastelands of the Sinai Peninsula — all because they saw themselves as grasshoppers!

In our time we hear a lot about complexes — inferiority complexes, superiority complexes, complexes about races, places, and things, and sometimes about not much of anything. To the long roster I would like to add one: The Grasshopper Complex. I'm not actually inventing a new complex — it has been around a long time; I'm merely giving it a name.

Victims of the Grasshopper Complex tend to fold up when confronted with any difficulty. Looking at an obstacle somewhere up ahead, they see themselves defeated before they even start, thinking of nothing except their own weaknesses. They won't tackle any task unless they are sure they are bigger than it is; they will not risk anything, especially defeat. They must be sure of victory before they begin the struggle, certain of winning before they will run the race. These are people who will match themselves against only the most trifling tasks, the most mediocre undertakings. For these I would like to propose a new Beatitude: Blessed are those who undertake something bigger than they are, and so stretch their souls, expand their horizons, deepen their lives, and strengthen their spiritual and moral muscles in struggle.

Really, though, I don't think such a Beatitude would be new. I am sure Caleb and Joshua knew about it 3,500 years ago. And thank God for those two fellows — and for their minority report. It went something like this: — Yes, the sons of Anak are in the land; we do not deny their presence there; we saw them, too. Of course the Nephilim are there; so what? We do not see ourselves as grasshoppers; we are men; we are God's men, and we are well able to take that land. Let's move; let's get up there; without delay, let's go.

The difference between the minority report and the majority was not in seeing the apparent facts; both saw the same set of these, viewing alike the circumstances in which they were. The difference was in *how they saw themselves*. Looking at the same situation, the same objective data if you please, ten men were scared half out of their wits, immobilized by fear — and two men weren't scared at all. "Do not fear them . . . We are well able to overcome," they said.

It is quite clear that Caleb and Johsua had a faith the other ten did not share, and that, by this faith, these two were seeing something the others did not see. It is obvious that they believed in themselves, that they believed in the others, in the whole assembly of Israel, and that they believed in God. No less than the other ten, these two recognized the immense difficulty of their task, but, unlike the others, they were ready to tackle it — because they firmly believed that working with them were vast resources of power. And they were right so to believe. Nobody, then or now, who has faith in God should ever think of him or herself as a grasshopper. Rightly understood, when God is with us we are no less powerful than God is.

To illustrate the truth of this, let me give you a simple little story which has been often told. It concerns a small boy who was trying to move a rather heavy stone in the back yard of the family home. His father came by, watched him for a few moments, and then said to his son, "Johnny, are you sure you are using all your strength?" Still heaving and puffing at his task, the boy answered, "Yes, Dad, I'm using all the strength I've got." Approaching and stooping down by him, his father said, "No, son, you are not using all your strength, for you have not yet asked me to help." With Father present and available, Johnny's resources of power were no less than the combined strength of himself and his father working together.

So it always is with God's people and their God. Caleb and Joshua knew this, and you and I should know it too. The truth is said so well in Isaiah 41:10 where God, through the prophet, gives this promise: "Fear not, for I am with you, be not dismayed, for I am your God; I will strengthen you, I will help you, I will uphold you with my victorious right hand."

Yes, I know that in our world in our time or any time there is much of which we might be afraid. But in the presence of any fearsome thing, we must understand that we have resources with which to overcome it. The secret of overcoming is not in closing our eyes to any frightful danger which may appear, but in opening them to the overwhelming resources which are at our command.

To a deeply troubled man Jesus once said, "Do not be afraid; only believe." (Mark 5:36; Luke 8:50) When you and I are troubled, my friend, wouldn't it be wonderful if we could hear Jesus saying this same thing to us? Well, I believe he is. He is saying: Faith is your alternative to fear; believe, and don't be afraid. If there is much against us, there is more with us.

And there is, in fact, much against us — there can be no doubt about that. Speaking of the moral struggle in which God's good people are forever involved, the Apostle Paul says, "We are not contending against flesh and blood, but . . . against the world rulers of this present darkness . . . against spiritual hosts of wickedness in the heavenly places." (Ephesians 6:12) That sounds as though the enemies whom we fight are formidable, and they are.

How do we fight them? In his very next sentence Paul tells us: "*Therefore*, take the whole armor of God . . ." You are going to need it; nothing less will do. You will need all the help you can get, all that God can give — the entire armament God can provide — not just a little of it here and there, but all there is.

Take this armor, Paul says, "that you may be able to withstand . . . and having done all, to stand." His picture of the armor is a vivid one: "Stand therefore, having girded your loins with truth, and having put on the breastplate of righteousness, and having shod your feet with the equipment of the gospel of peace; above all taking the shield of faith, with which you can quench all the flaming darts of the evil one . . ." All of this, Paul says, you need; and "above all," as he says, you need faith. The remainder of Paul's inventory of armament includes the "helmet of salvation" and "the sword of the Spirit, which is the word of God."

Paul's picture of the conflict in which we are wrestling is a picture of immense and awesome power on both sides. The moral struggle, the strife between right and wrong, is not a backyard game where children fire popguns and fall down and play dead, but, rather, the battle lines thunder with salvos from mightier guns than were ever assembled in any other war. The moral struggle is bigger than we sometimes think, with more against us and more with us than we often realize.

For that matter, whatever good land we would attempt to occupy, whether it be a matter of moral conquest or some other kind, we will find that the sons of Anak are there. Any land worth conquering has some leering giant. Whatever good place we strive to reach in life will have some muscular guardian standing at the gate and saying, "Thou shalt not pass." Out there in the big world is the immorality giant, the war giant, the alcohol and drug giant, and a lot of others, all of whom must be overcome before the good land of peace, order, and good will can ever be occupied. And here in our hearts, within our minds and spirits, where we must make conquest of ourselves, there are giants also. There are giants in the land of marriage, in the land of education, in the land of work — and any of these good lands which we would occupy must first be wrested from the giants.

Well, how do you feel about it? Do you think you can do it? Will you perhaps be like the ten spies who saw only the giants in the land and said, "We can't"? Or will you be like Caleb and Joshua who, seeing that they had some giants on their side, too, said, "We can"? Do you have the faith to believe in the giants that are with you, that are within you, even? Listen to the writer of 1 John who says, "Greater is he who is in you than he who is in the world." (4:4) He was writing to a persecuted and troubled Church; antichrist was already out there in the world, he said. The Christian forces seemed impossibly weak in comparison with all that stood against them. But today, after nearly 2,000 years, those persecuting and jeering giants are all long-time gone, but the Church remains.

Christ put his Church to work on this planet, giving his people their marching orders, their great commission: "Go into all the world . . . Make disciples of all nations." In other words, move — move in and occupy the land, go up and possess it in my name, says our Lord and Leader. And, concerning his Church and her prospects for the conquest, he said, "The powers of death (the gates of hell) shall not prevail against it." (Matthew 16:18)

But, ah! that small and heterogeneous group, those first Christians, who were they against the sons of Anak, against such bruising giants as Diocletian and Nero? Well, let me tell you who they were. They were persons who had come through Pentecost!

Jesus had said to his disciples, "You shall receive power when the Holy Spirit has come upon you." (Acts 1:8) The Spirit came and remarkable power was theirs. Before he went away from his disciples, Jesus had said (John 14:16), "I will pray the Father, and he will give you another Counselor (Comforter, Helper, Another to befriend you, One to stand by you)." The Greek word, so variously translated, is *Paraclatos*, meaning one who is called to stand alongside another.

Those first Christians were not alone, and they knew it. Jesus had said: The *Paraclatos* will come "to be with you for ever." Those people had the faith to believe that the *Paraclatos* would respond to their call to stand alongside them, and he did. And, my friend, if you and I have this faith, he will be here to stand alongside us also.

We began with this question of Jesus: "Why are you afraid? Have you no faith?" We conclude with this declaration of Jesus: "Do not be afraid; only believe." (Mark 5:36) Believe, and although your land of promise may be guarded by hostile giants and towering walls, you are "well able to overcome it." Believe, and although the sea may surge with storm around you, there is no peril which can ever paralyze you with fear.

A Barricade of Doors and a Bundle of Keys

Sixth Sunday after Pentecost

"Why do you make a tumult . . .?" — Mark 5:39

Oscar Wilde, who said many ridiculous things, among them said this: "Life is far too important a thing ever to talk seriously about." Oscar Wilde notwithstanding, I know of nothing that has been talked about more than life, both seriously and otherwise. Almost everybody who has ever said anything of importance about anything has had something to say about this human life of ours.

Some have been terribly cynical about it. One said that "life is a bridge of groans across a stream of tears," and Samuel Butler defined it as "one long process of getting tired." Pedro Calderon wrote that life is "a sentence man has to serve for being born," and another described it as "a terrible disease cured only by death." To Romain Rolland, life was seen as a "combat without grandeur, without happiness, fought in solitude and silence." Jonathan Swift said that life is "a ridiculous tragedy." H. L. Mencken changed that slightly, however, saying that life is "not a tragedy, but . . . a bore." "A bad bargain," said Montaigne on one occasion; "one long dirty trick," said Thorne Smith. Philosopher Arthur Schopenhauer, about the gloomiest of them all, wrote that life is "only a constant struggle for mere existence, with the certainty of losing it at last."

But not all have been overwhelmed by some glimpse of life's dark shadows. Some, thank God, have been able to look optimistically upon it and make some light-hearted comments about it. For example, there was Elbert Hubbard who defined life as "the interval between the time your teeth are almost through and the time you are almost through with your teeth!"

Of all the ways we may see life, however, I believe we see it most clearly when we look upon it as a journey, a going somewhere, a moving from this to that, from here to somewhere yonder, out of the past into the future — and, as for me, I see this journey as an adventure, dramatic, exciting. Yes, I know, as you do, that the going is not always easy. There are rough places along the trail, deep valleys, hard climbs, and sometimes long, dark nights through which we must grope our way onward. Sometimes the trail seems to run to the brink of a precipice or into the breast of an unscalable mountain. It seems sometimes that we have gone as far as we can, have done all we can do, that we must give up and give in to some powerful thing that stands in the way.

In the fifth chapter of Mark we are told about such a time in the experience of some people who lived in Palestine when Jesus did. Jarius was a powerful man; he was "one of the rulers of the synagogue." This man came rushing to Jesus, fell down at his feet, and said, "My little daughter is at the point of death." Have you ever had to say anything like that? If so, you know the feeling, that helpless feeling; so much you want to do something, and there is nothing you can do. You want to break through this moment, go beyond it, and take that little daughter with you to run and play again on spring's new grass or to roll in the autumn leaves. But you cannot; you can only stand and wait — while the fever rises and her beautiful young life ebbs away.

Well, Jesus had never had a little daughter to play on the spring grass or among the autumn leaves or smile her child's love into his eyes. But Jesus had other ways of knowing how Jarius felt — he seemed always to know what lay so deeply within the hearts of the people he met. So when Jarius said, "Come and lay your hands on her, so that she may be made well, and live," Jesus went. Before they reached the house of Jarius, however, there came persons to meet them, saying to Jarius, "Your daughter is dead." Then Jesus said to Jarius, "Do not be afraid; only believe," and he went on with him to the house.

There he "saw a tumult, and people weeping and wailing loudly." As he entered, Jesus said to the people, "Why do you make a tumult and weep? The child is not dead, but sleeping." The people laughed at him. But immediately then, with the child's mother and father, Jesus went into the room where she was, and taking her thin, pale hand into his hands, he said, "Little girl, I say to you, arise!" Do I need to finish the story? A door was opened that day; for Mr. and Mrs. Jarius and their little girl and their neighbors, the trail ahead opened up so they could travel on. Jarius could go on to his next duty in the synagogue; his wife could go on to tomorrow's chores about the house; and the child go on to play in the green grass of another spring.

Looking back at the whole of that episode from point of what we now know about it, can we not understand why Jesus, upon arriving at that house that day, asked his question of the people there: "Why do you make a tumult, and weep?" After all, ultimately, what was there to weep about? Jesus knew something which Jarius and his neighbors did not know; and I'm quite sure he knows some things we don't know. However, knowing him, we can believe.

Each of us, and every person in the world, is on a journey, going somewhere. For "three score years and ten," more or less, we will be journeying here, and then after that we will go on to finish the journey somewhere else. On our journey across this span of earthly years we travel forward on roads that are sometimes easy, sometimes difficult, and that seem sometimes to run into barricades we cannot pass. In this journey each traveler rather consistently confronts a barricade of doors and holds in his hand a bundle of keys.

It is sometimes difficult to breach a door that's closed and go on to what lies beyond. Obstacles stand in the way. Perhaps we want to achieve, to move on, to go up, but there are gates along the road, doors between this room of life and the next one — and these doors do not always open for us as we approach them. Sometimes we push and they will not budge, we try the latch and it will not move. And we are stopped, and we are very likely to make a tumult of our wailing and weeping.

But if there is ahead of us a barricade of doors, each of us also has a bundle of keys — our ways of dealing with the barriers, our means of overcoming the obstacles. The critical question is this: Will our keys fit the locks?

Some keys will unlock some doors and some will not. It's a funny thing about keys: they must fit — and a key that won't fit is as useless as no key at all. If we look, we can see around us on all sides people who are trying to open doors with keys that will not fit the locks.

We have a great many key vendors around, hawking their wares and urging us to buy this key or that. These hucksters are well aware that from time to time most of us come to doors that we would like to have open for us — we want to be where we have not yet arrived, we want what we do not yet have. The market for keys is a good market and the key-vending business can be a very profitable one. So the vendors appeal to us — they shout at us, they whisper to us, they paint pictures for us, they sing jingles into our ears.

An ad I saw in a newspaper, in its entirety and exact except for a name which I have changed, read this way: "Tired? Worried? Unhappy? Try Schneickelfritz's beer!" To be tired means that one needs something in the nature of recuperation and recovery before going on. And then, on top of that, to be worried, and in addition to being worried, to be unhappy — all of this amounts to quite a barrier to any normal kind of venturing into the tomorrows. So, having come to such a paralyzing impasse with life, what does one do? Well, one drinks Schneickelfritz's beer, of course! At least, if one listens to the huckster, one does. But the key won't fit.

In a community where I served as Pastor, we had a certain good citizen of middle age (whose name I could give you, but I think I should not). He was a busy man with several business interests, and there came a time when things were not going well for him, so he became tired, quite worried, and somewhat unhappy. He tried the Schneickelfritz key, and, of course, it didn't work. Never mind about that, though — the hucksters in all the nearby taverns kept plying him with their products. Becoming ill, he was in and out of hospitals several times, but no sooner out than he was back at a bar again. His bar buddies and bartenders knew about his liver and that the doctors had said he should never drink again. But this made no difference to the vendors; they killed him. For two years we watched him die, and then all the prominent citizens assembled for a funeral service, and we took his body out to the community cemetery and buried it. The key didn't fit — and let it be known that in the final rational moments before his death, this poor man was still tired, worried, and unhappy.

A large sign outside the office of a saving and loan company: "The road to a happy life starts here." To be more accurate, the sign might read: "Here is a good place to save your money." But to promise that your life will be happy just because you have saved your money is to promise too much; one can be miserly and miserable. The key of economic frugality does not necessarily unlock the door to happiness.

When you really look at it, some of this key vending business is ludicrous, laughable. You know the typical pitch: — Boys, do you want to be popular with the girls? Well, just use Chill Creme! (and here again I have changed a name). Just use this stuff on your hair and all your girl problems are solved! They'll all pursue you! You'll be irresistible! It won't matter if you have a bad disposition or if your manners are abominable; just put this stuff on your hair and this is all you will ever need to do! So they say — and thinking of all the implications, we smile about it. The solution is too easy; the key won't fit.

Girls, you want to be popular with the boys? Toothpaste! that's what you need! Why, it will transform you from the most forlorn, woebegone creature around into the most glamorous and popular person in town! Of course it must be a certain brand of toothpaste; no other will do. Or maybe it's Old Egypt eye shadow, or soap — some special kind of soap, of course.

Now I agree that it's a good idea to use soap and toothpaste; these products are good for washing bodies and cleansing teeth, but the key to getting along with other persons and being liked is not just in having well-groomed hair or a clean body or gleaming white teeth. Neatness and cleanliness are worthy objectives for their own sake, but to say that hair-dressing or soap is all we need for social success is to offer a key that will not unlock the door.

But the key vendors dangle their shining panaceas before us, promising almost everything but the moon and stars. "Aren't our keys pretty?" they say. "Look how bright they are, and how popular — almost everybody is using them." And so we take them and we try them. To get to where we think we want to be, we try force (because some say it will work); we try deceit (because some believe it's necessary); we try running over other people (because some contend one has to do this); we try laziness (because some argue that all success is just luck and effort makes no difference anyway).

And sooner or later, all of us who try these keys discover to our sorrow that while the keys might open some doors, they do not open the right ones, and we find ourselves stopped along the way, with life's highest fulfillments still somewhere ahead beyond unbreachable barricades.

Thank God, though, that most of us have in our bundles of keys some that do, in fact, take us far. If we have some sense of industry, some measure of courage, some spark of imagination, some genuine love of our fellow human beings, and some will to aspire, we can then walk with confidence up to many doors and know that we have keys which will open them. All of this means much in the course of the journey we make and provides a great deal of help to get us through.

But we need — and we deeply want — keys for all doors, ways to get beyond all barricades, including the last one, so that death itself at length does not stop us, but becomes simply an opening door through which we pass and from there go on. There are such keys, my friend. They are the Master's keys — master keys for all doors, if you please. Let me tell you about them.

A long time ago an old man, an outcast on a lonely island, waited and watched along the shores of the surrounding sea. His name was John, and in the final book of our New Testament he tells us something of what he saw. Early in his lifetime he had met one called Jesus and had followed him, walking with him among the hills of Galilee and along the roads of Judea, supping with him in the upper room, watching with him in Gethsemane, standing with him at Mount Golgotha, running to his emptied tomb the morning of his Resurrection. Across the ensuing years, at Ephesus and elsewhere, John had continued to stand with Jesus until in course of time his stance of faith had brought down the wrath of his opposition until now he was a prisoner on the Island of Patmos.

Across on the mainlands of Asia, Europe, and Africa, John's fellow Christians were experiencing hard times. Having been overthrown by Titus and his Roman legions, Jerusalem lay in ruins. Rome was pressing hard, and the followers of Christ were suffering severe persecution on every hand. Here on the rock cliffs of Patmos was this venerable man, shut off from his beloved people. Was he discouraged? afraid? uncertain of the future? By every rule of human measurement, he had reason to be.

But one day — it was the Lord's Day, he said — as he sat upon the cliffs looking, he saw something — a vision, an appearance, something. He looked into the heavens, saw a majestic glory — and the crucified and risen Christ at the right hand of the heavenly Father. He heard a voice; it was the voice of the Christ, and the voice said, "Fear not; I am the first and the last, the living one; I died, and behold I am alive forevermore, and *I have the keys* of Death and Hades." (Revelation 1:18)

"Alive forevermore!" Alive always. Alive in A.D. 90 when Rome was using the full force of her power to crush the life out of Christendom — but John was seeing the vision of an eternal Kingdom that would still be strong when great Rome had gone long since into the dust of ancient history . . . Alive in A.D. 425 when the Vandals were marching for the overthrow of the mightiest city of the world — but Saint Augustine in North Africa was writing his immortal testament of faith, *The City of God*, a book about a city that would never fall . . . Alive in A.D. 732 when the Saraceans came, and all of Europe trembled before the invader's crushing wave — but Charles Martel and his Gauls rose up from their altars, put on their armor, took up their spears, and went forth to turn the invader back on the battlefields of Tours . . . Alive in sixteenth century darkness when Martin Luther stood up in Central Europe to hold aloft a brighter light of faith by which he said the just should live . . . Alive in England's darkest days when John Wesley appeared and wrote and spoke, for half a century his relentless message burning like a fire through the rubbish of that nation's moral decay . . . And, moreover, and more importantly, *he is alive today!*

In our time there are cults and fads and isms of many varieties, most of them conspiring to divert us from the path or stop us where we are or turn us back from going on. If we are listening at all, we can hear a bedlam of voices, each in a different tongue, shouting to us, "I am the way . . . I am the key!" One says we must sit cross-legged and stare at our navels; another says we must stand on our feet and lift up our hands and say some magic words; another says we must sit around together in naked groups and tell one another every stupid thing we ever did or said or thought; and others say that we must draw pictures, or shoot ourselves with needles, or fill out questionnaires — and all of them promise us: This will do it for you, this will get you through to where you want to be.

And all the while, above it all, stands One of long-proven skill who says, "I am the way . . . I have the keys."

So we come back to the question Jesus asked long ago: "Why do you make a tumult?" When we come to the barricade which denies us passage to what lies beyond, why should we beat upon it with our fists and scream? One stands with us who says, "I have the keys," and even if all the keys in our own bundles fail to work, he has a key that will. After all, he has the keys of death itself — and if he can get us through that, he can get us through anything.

Don't Touch That Stone!

Seventh Sunday after Pentecost

And they took offense at him . . . — Mark 6:3

Much of what is written in the Gospels concerning Jesus is a reporting of his everyday meetings with the ordinary people of that place and time. In most ways those people were a great deal like us, and from these episodes of encounter we can learn invaluable lessons about our own relationships with him in our time.

Often we speak of Christ having come into our world, to our humankind, as though his coming were in some general, or remote, or somewhat ethereal sense. Not so. He came to real people on the streets where they lived; he met them at their work and their play, at their parties and their funerals, in their homes and their synagogues, in their times of heartache and of joy. He saw them as they were, sometimes kind, sometimes cruel. Sometimes when he came they received him gladly and sometimes they spurned him brutally.

If we read thoughtfully, we can often see ourselves on those streets of Capernaum and Jericho and Jerusalem; we can see ourselves mirrored in the people of Sychar or Cana or Bethany. And then, of course, there is Nazareth — and those people who lived in that town where Jesus grew to manhood and from which he went forth to move the world. One of the most revealing of the encounter stories is the report of what happened when Jesus came back from the other side of Galilee for a visit in his home community. We have the story in Mark 6:1-3:

> *He went away from there and came to his own country; and his disciples followed him. And on the sabbath he began to teach in the synagogue; and many who heard him were astonished, saying, "Where did this man get all this? What is the wisdom given to him? What mighty works are wrought by his hands! Is not this the carpenter, the son of Mary and brother of James and Joses and Judas and Simon, and are not his sisters here with us?" And they took offense at him.*

What a gold-mine of human interest is in this little story! Those people of that village were probably very good citizens, honest and reasonably upright, helpful to one another in times of trouble, good, God-fearing conventional types. But this young man Jesus — had he not grown up in their midst, played on their streets as a child, and later made tables and chairs for them in Joseph's shop? How could he be anyone special? He was indeed different; they recognized that "mighty works were wrought by his hands", that exceptional wisdom was his; and they said, "Where did this man get all this?"

They looked around among themselves, shook their heads, and decided: he could not have gotten it from us, not from this community. How very right they were about that: he had not gotten it from them — it had come from above. He is a local boy, we know this fellow, they said; and how very wrong they were about that — they really didn't know him at all. "Is not this the carpenter?" they asked. Yes, but he was more than that, and it was the "more than" which perplexed them so. They could readily admit that he was Jesus of Nazareth, but they were unable to understand how he could be anything more. He was an enigma to them, a puzzle, utterly unbelievable — so they did not believe.

If Jesus had grown up in your community, would you have believed? I doubt it. It's terribly difficult for most of us to accept the exceptional. Unable to explain Jesus, those people at Nazareth rejected him. Are not some of us guilty of doing the same thing? As we understand normality, we insist upon things being somewhat normal. And we have a persistent tendency to reject the person whose rise above the norm, or whose fall below it, is too much for us to comprehend or explain.

So a little later those people of Nazareth did what many of us would be inclined to do. As we are told in Luke 4:28-30, "they rose up and put Jesus out of their city, and led him to the brow of the hill on which their city was built, that they might throw him down headlong. But passing through the midst of them he went away." Later yet, when Jesus was in Jerusalem, other persons for the same reasons "took up stones to throw at him; but Jesus hid himself, and went out of the temple." (John 8:59) And even after that, as we read in John 10:31, the people "took up stones again to stone him."

We humans are terribly ready with our stones, aren't we? We are so quick to clobber whoever it is we do not understand, whether he is Christ standing strong for righteousness in the synagogue at Nazareth, or whether she is Mary bowed brokenly beneath the weight of her sins in the dusty streets of Magdala. Are we willing now to learn something from Jesus about this? To let him teach us, let us turn to another of his encounters with the people of his time. We read the account in John 8:3-11.

Jesus was in Jerusalem, at the temple there, and a huge crowd was present. Certain scribes and Pharisees brought to him a woman who had been caught in the act of adultery. Citing the law of Moses as their authority, they were ready to stone her to death. They said to Jesus, "What do you say about her?" For a little while Jesus said nothing in reply. Instead, he did a strange thing — he bent down and wrote with his finger on the ground. They persisted, insisting that Jesus give them an answer. At last he stood up, looked at them long and seriously, I think, and said quite simply, "Let him who is without sin among you be the first to cast a stone at her." Then once more Jesus bent down and wrote with his finger on the ground. As he did this, one by one the woman's accusers began to sneak away, beginning with the oldest among them. Presently, Jesus was left alone with the woman standing before him. He looked up, saw her there, arose, and said, "Where are they? Has no one condemned you?" The woman answered, "No one, Lord." And Jesus said, "Neither do I condemn you; go, and do not sin again."

Now, looking at this story, it is quite apparent that Jesus was in no way denying the evil of the woman's conduct; he was not approving what she had done — he was forgiving it. Jesus, of course, was hurt by her evil act, hurt, I suspect, infinitely more than were those scribes and Pharisees. But there was an immense difference between him and them. They would stone her and have done with the matter; he would forgive her and offer her another chance.

Jesus is letting us know that forgiveness is the pathway to redemption, that what stones cannot do, forgiveness can. He is teaching us, I think, that if we are to use redemptively and wholesomely the encounters we have with our fellow human beings, we must never, never approach them with stones in our hands, but rather with a readiness to forgive in our hearts and a purpose of trying to understand. I think I hear Jesus saying to me: If you are ever tempted to reach for a missile to hurl at someone, stay your hand! and *do not touch that stone!*

So, my friend, the message I share with you now is a simple one, the one I hear my Lord giving to me: Don't touch that stone! And there are three simple things I want to say about this.

First, the stone is there — a stone is within easy reach; you can easily stretch forth your hand to pick it up. Stones are numerous, for stones are of many kinds; not all of them are hard ball-sized lumps that fit snugly into a hand — some are hurled by the tongue. Things may be said or done which are more bruising than any real stone could ever be. Someone (and I have no idea who) has written eight little lines that hold a world of meaning. They go this way:

> Before I knew how cruel
> Just common talk can be,
> I thought that words were singing things
> With voices like the sea.
> Now that I've felt their caustic lash
> And know how they can sting,
> I hold my breath when they go by
> For fear they will not sing.

In all our relationships with our fellow-pilgrims in the venture and struggle of life's journey, we ought to remember always, as someone has said, that

> It takes only a little wound
> To bleed a dream to death,
> And love, too, may die,
> Deprived of but a single breath.

O yes, word-stones can have a devastating effect; they have been known on occasion to undo a lifetime of struggle in a few moments or a few days. Let me illustrate with a story, a true one.

A young physician, having just completed his medical training, moved into a small community and began to establish his practice there. Devotedly, he gave himself to the service of the people, working sometimes to the point of exhaustion, and often with little reward. One midnight he was called to the scene of a grisley automobile accident where two or three persons were dead and two or three others lay critically injured. As the doctor labored, doing what he could, running from one victim to another, a gathering crowd stood by and watched, as crowds will do. One man present had resisted the coming of so young a doctor to the community, and that night this man, watching the doctor work, said to two or three others that he believed the doctor was drunk. This report went across the community and almost everyone believed it. What nobody knew was that the young physician, immediately prior to that auto crash, had been at work for thirty-six hours with no sleep or rest. It was for this reason that he had staggered, as drunk, that night at the accident scene.

As a result of the word-stone that had been hurled (and having been hurled once had been picked up and hurled by others again and again), most of the young doctor's patients left him and very few new ones would trust him. More than two heartbreaking years of patient effort were required before he could regain the confidence of the people. Oh, how cruel, how brutal, such stones can be!

These word-stones occur in many guises and may be delivered in countless ways. One form is the outright falsehood, the deliberate lie. And then there are half-truths, and there is double-talk, and there are innuendos and mere suggestions. And words can be made to play tricks. For instance, an archbishop from Europe, arriving in New York, was asked by a news reporter if he planned to visit any night clubs in this country. Believing the question a bit of good-humored banter, he replied in kind, "Are there night clubs in New York?" And, would you believe it? the newspaper headline read this way: Archbishop Inquires about New York Night Clubs.

When Gifford Pinchot was governor of Pennsylvania more than a generation ago, there was a family pet, a dog, which was cared for for a while within the walls of the state penitentiary. Somebody, just for the fun of it, wrote a whimsical story about the dog having committed some misdeed and having been sentenced to prison. The governor's opponents managed to twist the story in such a way that the episode became for years a heavy millstone around his political neck.

Yes, for anyone who can talk, there is a stone within easy reach. But don't touch it.

The next thing I wish to say concerning the stone is that there's someone at whom to throw it. Anybody with a mind to throw stones can always find a target. That target may be any perfectly fine and wonderful person — for one who will stoop to throwing stones is usually not very discretionary about the persons at whom the stones are thrown. When a person makes himself judge, jury, and executioner, no person is exempt from his condemnation. And, sadly, some folks seem chronically disposed to throw stones, and if they cannot find one target they will find another. They go about, heaven forgive them, with hands full of stones, and their throwing them is more a matter of how they feel within themselves than a matter of justice or fairness toward those at whom the stones are thrown. So duck, everybody! — And pray that hearts will soften and hands unclench and that stones will fall to the ground.

Another target may be the person who has a shortcoming, a peculiarity, a defect, someone who in some way is different from us. I once knew an alert and intelligent girl of junior high school age who from birth had suffered the disfigurement of a hair-lip, and the other girls, by their tauntings and teasings, stoned her — almost to the death. Sheer brutality, this.

Yet another target may be one who has blundered, failed, made a mistake, done a stupid or foolish thing — or sinned. And people do, you know. But if you see someone who has tripped and fallen, is it fair to throw stones at him? Would it not be better to rush to his side and try to help him to his feet again? Ask yourself this: No matter how wrong that fellow is, will he be helped if I throw stones at him? Will my stoning cause him to "go and sin no more"? Will it help to give him another chance?

Yes, anybody with an inclination to throw a stone can always find a target. But don't throw it! Leave it there on the ground; don't even reach down and pick it up. Keep your hands free to reach out and help someone, to reach out in warm caress, to reach out in sympathetic and understanding embrace. It is awfully difficult to hug somebody when your hands are filled with stones.

The third thing I would mention to you I will put in the form of a question: Who are you, who am I, that we should cast that stone anyway? "The one who is without sin among you," said Jesus, let him cast it. This limits the throng of stone-casters greatly, doesn't it? Jesus did not say, "He whose sin is less than this woman's, let him be the first to cast a stone at her," but "he who is without sin." The trouble is that too often we think we may stone the person whose sins (in our opinion, mind you) are more sinful than ours or somehow different from ours. Interesting, isn't it? — other people's kinds of sins are the ones we would rather cast our stones at.

Jesus did not tell those men at the Jerusalem temple that they should not stone the woman; he simply drew the lines of eligibility, told them who was qualified — and none were. Deeply knowing this, guiltily one by one, they dropped their stones. They had come carrying them, ready. But each man, sneaking a look about him to see who was watching, dropped his stone and turned away.

Well, those men were not the last ones in all history to carry their stony arsenals in readiness for the kill. Others have, and some still do. How about you — and me? Let us note this: there in that ancient street Jesus stooped and wrote something on the ground. What he wrote no person knows, and perhaps no one ever will. But I have the feeling that he is writing still — and, while writing, waiting for us to decide what we will do about the stones we have in our hands.

And here we are — today. Open your hand and look at it. Carefully now, thoughtfully. Is a stone there? If so, drop it and leave it here, right here. If you are coddling that with which you would clobber somebody, turn it loose, let it go. What better place to leave it than before the altar of the Lord's church? Whatever you bring when you come, never go away carrying any stones in your hands.

One Sunday morning several years ago I suggested this to the congregation of the church where I was pastor. On Monday I found on my desk a memo from the office secretary. This is what she had written: "I have asked the custodian to pick up all those stones in the sanctuary. I think there are a great many." Not at the moment having good presence of mind, I read the note with much anxiety. Have rocks been thrown through our windows during the night? I wondered. I rushed into the sanctuary to see what the damage was, only to find everything quite in order. Presently, encountering the secretary, I said to her, "What's all this about stones?" She looked at me for a long half-minute, and then said, "Don't you remember your sermon yesterday morning?" When I blushed a little in embarrassment, she said, "I was just trying to tell you that a lot of 'stones' that were brought in here yesterday were not carried away when the people left." So it ought to be, always.

You see, we are of the Christian faith and the Christian church; we are disciples of the Christ. And the Spirit of the Church is not the spirit of the world; the Spirit of the Church is the Holy Spirit of God. As the Church, we are in business with Christ, and our business is redemption, our work to behave redemptively toward every person. And this behavior pattern has no place in it for throwing stones.

So let's drop them; let's leave them where we are; let's not carry them around with us any longer. Let's rid ourselves of the burden of them, free our hands that we may stretch them out in loving reach to all. And, my dear friend, if ever in your tomorrows you meet someone at whom you might throw a stone, and somewhere near you discover a stone that you might throw, remember this: Do not ever, ever touch that stone!

Tending the Gardens of God

Eighth Sunday after Pentecost

So they went out and preached . . . — Mark 6:12

It has been aptly said that we Christians are the summoned and the sent. We have been summoned by Christ to come out of the world to him, and then by him we are sent back into the world again. He bids us come, and then he bids us go and do his bidding. This is beautifully illustrated in Mark 6:7-13 by an event from the time of Jesus. We read: "He called to him the twelve, and began to send them out . . . So they went out and preached . . ."

It is amply clear that in calling us to come to him Jesus has two purposes in view. He invites you and me to come to him so that, first, he may help us and, second, so that he may send us out in his name to help others. "Come to me" and "Go into all the world" — these two instructions of Jesus must be read alongside one another.

"Come to me, all you who labor and are heavy laden, and I will give you rest." (Matthew 11:28) "If anyone thirst, let him come to me and drink." (John 7:37) As he invites us to come to him, Jesus is making very real promises of personal help to us as we accept his invitation — to the weary, rest; to the thirsty, drink. Then, having come to him, we hear his other words: "Go therefore and make disciples of all nations . . . teaching them to observe all that I have commanded you." (Matthew 28:19-20) "You shall be my witnesses . . . to the end of the earth . . ." (Acts 1:8)

Our Lord cares about you. But to say this is also to say that he cares about every other person; for who are you? When I say that he cares about you, "you" might just as well be someone else. When I say he cares about you, I could say with equal truth that he cares about the person next to you or the person on the other side of the earth, for all of you are persons of humankind, members of this race he loves, to whom he comes, for whom he dies, and for whose sakes he everlastingly lives.

When (probably through the encouragement of some other person) we have come to Christ, he desires then that we should go to others. No, perhaps not as missionaries to some other quarter of the globe (although it may possibly be so), but that we do our living, wherever we are, in loving and thoughtful care for all who are around us. One of the most exciting discoveries we Christians can make is to realize what our *relationships* are, not only with our Lord, but also with all other persons whose lives are ever touched by ours.

Now, if I may, I would like to make this wonderful scope of truth come alive for you in a picture, a kind of analogy, a figure of speech. I want to speak about gardens, and in doing this, I am speaking about what the Church is, who we are — and I am speaking about an exciting dimension of our relationship.

Gardens are places where things grow. And I think that God certainly must love a garden — gardens of growing things. He has spangled history with gardens of beauty, and much of history has hinged in gardens. The Genesis account of this earthly race of ours begins in a garden, and there in that garden the first scene of our earthly drama is played out. In quaint simplicity we are told that "the Lord God planted a garden in Eden, in the east, and there he put the man whom he had formed." (Genesis 2:8)

Much later there was a garden called Gethsemane where the drama reached one of its mountain-top moments when at one mid-eastern midnight the Savior of the world wrestled in self-giving prayer. And nearby on the slopes of Mount Golgotha was another garden, and in that garden a new-made tomb, where nearly 2,000 years ago, at the dawning of a "first day morning," occurred the most extraordinary event in the whole history of the world.

It would appear that, from the first, God has placed his people in gardens — and always for a purpose. In the Genesis story, what is the commission which God gives to his people there? "Be fruitful . . . multiply . . . subdue the earth . . . have dominion . . ." (Genesis 1:28) This suggests that the gardener's assignment is not to exploit or deplete what is placed in his care, but to develop and help to bring it to its very best. In the realm of nature this can be quite a task; and you know at least something of this task if you have ever worked a vegetable garden, attempting to keep the weeds away so the tomatoes and beans will have a chance to grow.

There is a difference between a garden and a wilderness. A wilderness might have a wild kind of beauty, but it is unproductive; a garden, on the other hand, has an ordered kind of beauty, and it is productive. And what makes the difference between a wilderness and a garden? Just this: *the presence of the gardener, the labor of someone who cares.*

For many years the story has been told of the country preacher who was riding horseback along a rural road in his community when he came upon a man of his parish working with a hoe in his garden at the roadside. The preacher said, "Brother Jones, you ought to thank God for all the beautiful squash and potatoes and other nice things you have growing there in your garden." To which Brother Jones replied, "Yep, suppose so, Preacher, but you should have seen this patch of ground last year when the Lord had it all by himself!"

You see, wherever God would have a garden, there he would put a person with tools of toil in his hands.

But, my dear friend, God's gardens are not in distant Edens only, nor are they gardens of physical growth alone. *God has other gardens, gardens of another kind,* where growth is more spiritual than physical. These gardens are in the hearts of men and women and boys and girls, *his people.* This is where, in fact, his most cherished gardens are, and here *in these gardens* he would have love bloom, beauty flower forth, a glory spring into life. And for this kind of gardening *he needs his gardeners also* — and you are one of them and I am another.

Think with me now, please, about our work as gardeners for God, about our tending these gardens, trying to grow the good, to cultivate the best, to produce the most in the souls and spirits and minds of the people for whom God cares.

In nature the only food-producing factory is in the leaves of living plants. Here the process of photosynthesis brings together the power of the sunlight and the nurture of the earth; here the material resources of earth and sky are caused to meet and combine and make something which otherwise would not be. Likewise, the only place in this world where moral and spiritual beauty and value are produced is within human beings, within us. Spiritual and moral qualities are not generated "out there" somewhere in the ether. Here within us are brought together that which comes down from God, the good grace of heaven, and that which rises up from the well-spring of our humanity, and of these something new is made, as Paul said, "a new creation" in Christ (2 Corinthians 5:17).

And you and I, we of this faith, we of the church, are engaged in this production. We are involved in a dynamic action drama. Looking again at the story of beginnings, one must be impressed that when God planted his garden in Eden he started something — physical life for man, the spiritual creature — but there came a spiritual blight and beauty was bruised, the garden was marred, and the man and the woman went out, wandering somewhere yonder. But God sent his Son, pursuing man, offering life, restoration, and return, and so were we pursued all the way to a place called Calvary; and there he overtook us, met us at the point of our deepest hurt, our sin — and ever after he has been with us, laboring to give life, restore beauty, produce love in the soul gardens of his people everywhere. He calls us to work with him, to be his gardeners in his gardens.

Our role as gardeners is, of course, a helper role. So is the role of the gardener who grows tomatoes, for that matter; he really doesn't *grow* them, he simply fixes things so growth can happen. If at your home you have a garden in your backyard, you cut out the weeds, you stir the soil, you destroy the cutworms, you spray against the blights and the parasites — you try to arrange things so nature can have a chance to do its work.

Well, you do have a garden, more than one, actually. You have the garden within you — and it needs some attention. And you have some gardening responsibility in the lives of all the persons you touch. But along with the gardener's responsibility, you also have the gardener's privilege, and great indeed it is. Your privilege it is to plant, plant seeds of good and of good example, seeds of encouragement and inspiration. Your privilege it is to water, to provide nurture, to nourish and strengthen and support. Your privilege it is to protect, to shield and shelter God's gardens from their enemies, to fight, as it were, the beetles, the blights, and the parasites, and to fence out, insofar as you can, the varmints that would destroy.

All this, let us never forget, is for us responsibility as well as privilege. Never should we stand indifferently by while moral compromise and corruption sweep through our land like a sickness. Perhaps neither you nor I can do dramatic or spectacular things to assure that the children of our community have their chance to grow up without constant exposure to the contagion of some mortal moral disease. But we can do something — you can, and I can — and what we can do we dare not leave undone. Maybe we cannot do it all, but we can help, and to the limits of our power, we'd better be about it. Yes, ours is only a helper role, but, in heaven's name, let's be the helpers we are called and sent to be.

For a year and a half the Apostle Paul had been at Corinth — preaching and teaching — planting, cultivating, laboring. Apollos and Peter had also been there, and divisions had developed among the Corinthians concerning these men. Writing to them in regard to this controversy, Paul had this to say: "I planted, Apollos watered, but God gave the increase." (1 Corinthians 3:6) Each man had made some contribution toward a set-up in which God could get his work done. No one person can do everything, but anyone can help

— a Paul can plant, an Apollos can water — and then God can produce the growth, the growth of the good, of life, beauty, and love in these gardens that mean so much to him.

Together we are the Church, you and I and some millions of other persons who are, like us, the disciples of Christ in our time. An important part of our function in our world (or God's world, if you please) is to provide a fertile seedbed where fragile life can put down its roots and grow. World-wide, nation by nation, community by community, city block by city block, home by home, a major concern of ours must always be to maintain the kind of living conditions which will best support the loftiest and noblest development of individual human persons.

In various branches of science a "culture" is a biological or bio-chemical "set-up" which produces micro-organisms. In human society a "culture" is an intellectual, spiritual, moral, and legal "set-up" which produces types of persons, "ways of life," patterns of thought, forms of behavior, and modes of relationship — and these can differ vastly from one culture to another.

Well, the Christian community, the Church, is a "culture" also, is a "set-up" producing something. The Christian "culture," when true to its character, is a producer of the good and the beautiful in human life. A primary purpose of this "culture" is to provide the incentive, the direction, and the nurture which will most encourage the finest flowering of the human mind and spirit.

In an earlier day of radio in America, one of the most successful religious programs came out of Indianapolis. It was the work of E. Howard Cadle, and the program originated in Cadle Tabernacle in that Indiana city. For a good number of years each of those broadcasts identified the purpose of the program with these words: "Making your community a place where it is easier to do right and harder to do wrong." This, I believe, is a worthy objective of the church of Jesus Christ in any community and across the world. Our role in the world, in part at least, is to be makers of environment, to surround growing persons with what helps them grow.

In a large American city a little girl was lost from her parents. Finding the child wandering about and crying for her mother, a kind policeman took her to the precinct station, where loving words and a little ice cream soon dried away the tears. But the little one was not able to tell the police people who she was — only that her name was Mary, but her last name she did not know, nor could she tell the address of the house where she lived. As her police station friends contined to ask their questions in the hope that there would be some clue to her identity, the child suddenly brightened and said, "If you could take me to my church, I can find my way home from there." This, my dear fellow-churchman, is what the Church ought to be, and, when genuine, this is what the Church is — that place from which a little child can find her way home, that place from which, after the growing of the years, she can find her way to the heavenly Father's house at last.

Please hear me now: every one of us — in church, at home, at work, at play, in the daily routines of our living wherever we are — is doing something in somebody's garden. And there is much we may do — to help or to hinder. Jesus had a considerable amount to say concerning what we ought to be in relationship with other persons. "Witnesses to me," he said. "You are the light of the world," he said (Matthew 5:14) — and to be light is to give support to life, for this is what light does. "You are the salt of the earth," he said (Matthew 5:13) — and to be salt is to provide a deterrent against decay, for this is what salt does, preserving, for instance, meats and other foods which otherwise would rot and be ruined.

You see, Christ has given to you and me some essential roles to play in the majestic drama of what God is doing in his world. His gardens are everywhere, and in the walk and work of life we touch them daily. What is it we are doing to them? What is the effect of our touch? Sometimes we more than touch them — we *enter* them; in the ongoing experience of joy and pain, success and failure, rising and falling, it often happens that one enters into the life of another.

With what reverence we should walk there! With what thoughtful care we should move along the garden pathways of another person's life! Some I have known to move like bulldozers, rending and tearing; others I have seen go with watchful tread and reach with gentle touch and surgeon's skill to mend and heal and help. These gardens are committed to us, in part at least, for our tending care, and surely it is with care we should attend them.

One of the much loved hymns of Fanny Crosby has this stanza:

Down in the human heart, crushed by the tempter,
Feelings lie buried that grace can restore;
Touched by a loving heart, wakened by kindness,
Chords that were broken shall vibrate once more.

This, my dear fellow-Christians, is who we are — menders of broken chords, so that hearts may sing again. We are gardeners, you and I, and these gardens need our attention, cry out for our care.

The good gardener sees the seasons come and go, and in each season sees his duty and does it — in the flowering of spring, the growing of summer, the wilting frost of autumn, and the cold bleak of winter. In the changing seasons of a human lifetime the inward garden of spirit and soul and mind will need in many varied ways the skillful touch of the gardener's gentle hand.

Sometimes the gardener's labor is a pleasant chore — when rain and sunshine are nicely mingled and growing things are doing well. Sometimes, though, the gardener's task is hard, with a great deal of strain and pain. But do remember this about the gardener: the gardener is one who always cares — and for one who loves a garden, gardening is never a drudgery, but always a joy.

Sinners in the Hands
of a Loving God

Ninth Sunday after Pentecost

And he had compassion on them . . . — Mark 6:34

On February 3, 1943, in the midst of World War II, an American transport ship named S.S. Dorchester was torpedoed and sunk in the frigid waters of the North Atlantic. On board that vessel were four military chaplains, two Protestant, one Roman Catholic, and one Jewish. Having given away their own life jackets and done all they could to help others, those four men sacrificed themselves, dying together as the Dorchester went down. When last seen, the four were standing, arms interlocked, on a sloping water-washed deck, their lips moving in unison as they pronounced the immortal words of the Lord's Prayer.

One of these men was Clark Poling, age 32, minister son of an esteemed minister father, Dr. Daniel A. Poling. Following his son's death, Dr. Poling told of the last time he saw Clark. As Dr. Poling told it, the young chaplain walked into his father's study and said, "Tell me, Dad, what do you know about God?" Dr. Poling replied, "Son, I'm afraid I don't know very much, but what I know I know for sure." Then for a long time the two men sat together and talked.

Well, friend, let me ask you a question: What do you know about God? Not much perhaps; but I do hope there are some things which you know for sure. What most of us know about God we have found out from our Lord Jesus Christ. And why not? For, after all, we read in 2 Corinthians 5:19 that "God was in Christ." And in 2 Corinthians 4:6 we are told that we are given "the light of the knowledge of the glory of God in the face of Jesus Christ." If we look long at Christ, if we listen to him, if we watch him, we learn as John did (1 John 1:5), that "God is light," and (1 John 4:8) that "God is love."

One of the stories Mark tells of Jesus pictures his landing when he and some of his disciples had crossed by boat from one side of

Galilee to the other. There, Mark says, Jesus "saw a great throng, and he had compassion on them . . ." (Mark 6:34) Compassion: this is the way Christ was, compassionate. This is the way God is, compassionate, loving. Because of what we see in Christ, in this particular I think we can be very sure of God.

I invite you to think with me now on this topic: Sinners in the Hands of a Loving God. I believe this title relates to all of us, you and me and all others of humankind — for all have sinned. But there is another fact, a very wonderful one: all are in God's hands. A song we've often heard puts it this way: "He's got the whole world in his hands . . . the little tiny baby . . . you and me, brother." It's true; he has.

So, God being who he is and we being who we are, "Sinners in the Hands of a Loving God" is a totally suitable subject for our thought. But be sure to underline the word "loving," for it is this word which pictures the *kind of God* in whose hands we are, and if we are in his hands it is of supreme importance to us what kind of God he is.

Perhaps you have heard of a very famous sermon entitled, *Sinners in the Hands of an Angry God.* That sermon was preached by Jonathan Edwards at Enfield, Connecticut, on July 8, 1741. Take note of the adjective in that title: angry — an angry God, not loving; he is, as it were, a God of a different kind.

Jonathan Edwards was a renowned preacher, a master of the English language, a Puritan theologian who believed in a God who saves people and damns people more or less at will, who does with immortal souls what pleases him, rescuing some from the burning and letting the rest drop into the fires of hell. So on that July day in 1741 this fellow Edwards, one time the president of Princeton University, put the worst of fatalistic dogma into the best of colonial English and for an hour dangled his audience like puppets over the burning brimstone. He painted luridly vivid scenes of souls plunging into the fiery lake — because they had fallen into the hands of an angry God.

People screamed and cried out, they wailed and wept, seizing the pews and clinging to the church pillars with white-knuckled hands, desperately trying to hold onto something, as they could veritably feel themselves plunging down into the fires of hell with no hope and no escape. Edwards pictured the wrath of God as great waters dammed and ready to break, as an arrow fitted in the bow, aimed, and ready to fly straight into the heart of each object of the divine indignation.

Now, I have read and re-read this sermon, and I want to tell you this: Nowhere in it can I find the name "Jesus"; nowhere can I find the title "Christ"; and the word "love" does not appear. The sermon is a declaration of doom, having no redemption in it, no offer of hope.

Yes, sinners are indeed in the hands of God — I agree. But I want to change the adjective from "angry" to "loving." I prefer to see God as Jesus represented him; I will choose the God I see in Christ, the God who "so loved the world that he gave his only Son that whoever believes in him should not perish, but have eternal life" (John 3:16). I prefer to see God as the biblical prophet portrayed him when he said, "Thou art a God ready to forgive, gracious and merciful, slow to anger and abounding in steadfast love . . ." (Nehemiah 9:17).

So, with due apology to Brother Edwards, I would like us to see the other side, the real character, of this God in whose hands we are. I am fully aware that this sermon may not prove to be the perfect homiletical masterpiece that the Edwards sermon was, and I am quite sure this preacher will never be a president of Princeton University! There is also another difference — of interest to you, I suspect; this sermon will not be as long as that one! Nor is it likely to be remembered in history as that one has been. But I don't care about that: I care about us — and I'd like us to have a little better picture of the God who has us in his hands. For as I examine my own life, I strongly suspect that if God had been of an angry disposition, he could have found good reason to have clobbered me into the dust a long while ago. The fact that he has been good to me is to me convincing evidence that he has the patience of a great, great love.

What I want to say is this: As a sinner, I know of no hands in which I would rather be than God's. He loves me, and I can trust him to act in the interest of what is best for me, to forgive me and help me get beyond the sins of the past, to overcome, to be strong against them. I know many wonderful people — generous, thoughtful, kind; but I would rather rest my case with God than with anyone else I know. People may or may not be always patient, loving, and forgiving, but on these issues God never fails.

Because a small boy had been somewhat naughty during the day, his mother put him to bed early that night. As she was about to turn out the light and leave the room, she said, "Now, Jimmie, it's time to say your bedtime prayer." But her son objected, "No, Momma," he said, "not now. You go away and then I will say it." His mother, thinking of his misbehaviors, asked, "Jimmie, do you want to tell God something you don't want me to hear?" "No, Momma," said Jimmie, "it isn't that; it's just that if I tell you about things, you will keep remembering and reminding me of them, but if I tell God he will forget about it and never remind me again.''

I believe Jimmie understood something about which the Bible is quite clear — that our God will bury our sins to the depths of the sea, remove them from us as far as the East is from the West, and remember them against us no more. Other persons are not always so kind. You have heard the expression "bury the hatchet." A hatchet, of course, may be an instrument of conflict, a weapon, and to bury it is to suggest that the conflict is over. But, unfortunately, not many people ever forget where they bury a hatchet, and, remembering, they go about digging up the rusty old things that should be left buried and long forgotten. When some offense occurs, the offended person will sometimes say that all is forgiven, and so it seems to be — until the occurrence of some new tension becomes the occasion for digging up all the old carnage and dragging it out again.

You have heard also, I suppose, the expression "Indian giver." (It is used in reference to persons who give and then take back the gift.) Many people do this — their giving is so conditional. But you count on the gifts of God to be of the unconditional kind; when he gives, it's for keeps. He does not give his love only to withdraw it again.

Like his loving gift at Bethlehem and Calvary, all his gifts are lasting, permanent; they are never conditioned upon how they are received or what happens afterward. When God gave his Son at Bethlehem, he did not then withdraw the gift when people proved ungrateful, when they spat upon the Christ and put a crown of thorns on his brow and drove nails into his hands and feet. The heavenly Father did not take back his gift when the giving became inhumanly painful in the Garden of Gethsemane or on the summit of Mount Golgotha.

I am certain God has the power to clobber anybody anytime, but he is a loving God, and he doesn't do it. He might have sent a few lightening bolts into that crowd outside Pilate's praetorium and silenced its brutal cry, "Crucify! Crucify!" But he did not. Many people, it seems, stand ready to use all the power they've got over almost anyone within reach; but it is not so with God — he has power he doesn't use.

In Gethsemane, when they came to seize Jesus and take him away, one of his disciples drew a sword, but Jesus said to him, "Put your sword back into its place." I do not want the defense of your sword, said Jesus. Then he explained that, if he should choose, he could call more than twelve legions of angels to his defense (Matthew 26:53). He was talking about *power*, a lot of power, measured not in megatons but in angel-units.

What just one of those angels, by lifting just one little finger, could have done in Jerusalem the day Christ was crucified! What havoc, what devastation, what panic among the throngs along the Via Dolorosa and on the slopes of Mount Calvary! What a flying of phylacteries and swords! But it did not happen. A loving heavenly Father was giving his Son — all the way to death — and lashings and thorns and nails notwithstanding, he was not about to withdraw his gift.

God being like he is, it is no wonder that we read in Scripture again and again about his "everlasting love" — for his is a love that can outlast anything, can survive all rejection, can endure every hurt. When it comes to a matter of being patient with sinners, there is no other patience like the patience of God.

Once when the people of a Palestinian village rejected Jesus and his party, James and John said, "Lord, do you want us to bid fire come down from heaven and consume them?" The two errant disciples were manifesting an impatient spirit of "get even." But Jesus rebuked them, reminding them that this is not God's way, saying to them, "You do not know what manner of spirit you are of." (Luke 9:54) God doesn't react every time a sinner does some stupid thing; we usually do, but he doesn't. Instead, he gives his love and patiently awaits the sinner's response to it.

It is true: many people do not know how to handle sinners; but God does. God has had sinners on his hands for a long time, many of them, and I'm sure that again and again he has been terribly disappointed with his human creatures. According to the Genesis account, the very first one went bad on him, sneaked off into a shadowed corner; but God came looking for him, saying, "Adam, where are you?" (Genesis 3:9) And ever since Adam's time, it would appear, his progeny have been wont, like him, to wander into the shadows.

But God comes loving and looking, seeking and saving. Look at history, if you please. Observe how God has pursued us, has come after us, has put up with our shenanigans, grieved over our follies, been offended by our ingratitude and hurt by our sins, and yet through it all he has given us chance after chance and has not wiped us off this little planet. As I survey history, trace the dealings of God with our humanity, I cannot find a place anywhere in the long chain of events where God began to be an angry God. Yes, he has been grieved, offended, hurt; but the action patterns of our Lord are not those of one who is angry. He was talking love and forgiveness in the time of Isaiah and Hosea and Christ — and he still is today.

No, and make no mistake about this, God does not "wink" at our sins; he doesn't look the other way or close his eyes. Our sins DO make a *difference* with God. And please understand this: because of our sins, he has done some things differently; he has done some things because of our sins which obviously otherwise he would not have done. Do not overlook the fact that it was "on account of sins" that Christ came, that Christ suffered, that Christ died.

No, God does not retaliate when a sin is committed against him; he doesn't try to get even with us in some way. If he did, having the power he has, I am sure my first sin would have been my last, for never would I have had the chance to commit a second one. Praise God for his patient endurance; he does not react to our various and sundry sinful actions.

Instead, he makes one all-comprehensive response to the whole sin of all mankind. He sends the Savior; he offers forgiveness; he provides salvation for every penitent and responding sinner in all time. And this, my dear friend, I cannot believe is the act of an angry God, but of a God who, Christlike, is loving and compassionate.

In what way, then, does God deal with sinners? What is our Lord's response to our sins? What is it that he has done? Answer: God has NOT made a bigger club with which to beat us down; instead, he HAS sent redeeming love by which to lift us up.

No, our God does not ignore the fact that we are sinners; he is responsive; and he responds not with a club, but with a Gift — one Gift Supreme, and then the many varied gifts of his abounding grace. If you are a sinner, friend, you are in the hands of God — but he is not an angry God; you are in the hands of a God who loves you. This God marshalls the finest resources of heaven and sends his best to earth, doing all he can to keep us OUT of whatever fire Jonathan Edwards was dangling us over.

If we can see ourselves as "sinners in the hands of a loving God," I believe we are in a good position to make our response to that love. In this position we admit that we are sinners and we confess our faith that the whole power of the Eternal is lovingly directed to our good, to our redemption and our release from the captivity of all the lesser powers that hold us. "Lesser" powers, do I say? Yes: Great is the strength of sin; but one power is greater: the loving and life-lifting grace of our wonderful Lord.

We do him wrong whom we have hurt by our sins to say that he is angry. Most of us would be — if we had been so hurt. But this God, who, although so hurt, can be so kind and patient, surely he must be the loving Lord, for the things that God has done and does are the kinds of things that only love can ever do. As a sinner, I know of no place I would rather be than in the hands of this God who loves me.

And how great is this love! The stirring language of an unknown poet (or poets, some think) says it well:

> The love of God is greater far
> Than tongue or pen can ever tell;
> It goes beyond the highest star
> And reaches to the lowest hell.
>
> Could we with ink the oceans fill,
> And were the sky of parchment made,
> Were every stalk on earth a quill,
> And every man a scribe by trade,
>
> To write the love of God above
> Would drain the oceans dry,
> Nor could the scroll contain the whole,
> Though stretched from sky to sky.
>
> O love of God, how rich and pure!
> How measureless and strong!
> It shall forevermore endure,
> The saints' and angels' song.

God's Accessory People

Tenth Sunday after Pentecost

"There is a lad here . . ." — John 6:9

Would you like to be someone of importance in the world? You can, each of us can — and I want to speak with you about this. I want to speak with you of something wonderful every one of us can be. However old or young, however rich or poor, however educated or unlearned, however skilled or inept, all of us can be *God's accessory people*. We can be persons of significance, participants in high venture, players in the enormous and wide-ranging drama of what God is doing on our human scene in our time.

Do you remember an episode on a hillside above the Sea of Galilee when Jesus was teaching there? We read about it in John 6:1-15. It is the famous story of the feeding of the 5,000. One of the principals in this episode was a small boy — a lad, John calls him. The boy had come to that place because he had heard that Jesus would be there, and I suppose he wanted to see Jesus and hear him. Apparently the crowd was made up mostly of men, this lad being the only boy who is mentioned, and we do not know much about him, not even his name. Where he was standing we are not told — perhaps, bashfully, at the fringe of the crowd, or maybe eagerly somewhere up close to Jesus.

We know, though, that when there was need for food, and when a kind of survey was made, Andrew came to Jesus and said, "There is a lad here . . ." Not just any sort of lad was he, but one who had thoughtfully brought food with him when he came, five barley loaves and two fishes, his lunch, I suppose. So far as we are told, his was the only food among that whole assembly of people. Now precisely in what way that little bit of food was put into the hands of Jesus we do not know, but it was. Perhaps Andrew or one of the other disciples went to the boy and asked him if he would give up his lunch basket; if so, he did.

There was, however, a general discussion of the problem of feeding the people, and perhaps the boy heard of the need for food and voluntarily brought his basket to Jesus without being asked to do so. It is quite probable that when Andrew said, "There is a lad here," the boy was standing already at Andrew's elbow facing Jesus, his basket of loaves and fishes uplifted so Jesus could reach and take them. In whatever way it came about, the boy willingly, and perhaps eagerly, gave the food he had.

Then he sat down with the rest of the multitude and watched as Jesus distributed those five barley loaves and two fishes among 5,000 people. Speaking of those loaves and fishes, Andrew had said, "What are they among so many?" Very little, actually, as we all know. But somehow in the hands of the Master they became much, enough, and all the people were fed. I do not know how Jesus did this; but then I do not have to know. I know him — and if he does some things I cannot explain, I shall then but bow the more deeply in his presence and hold him in the higher reverence.

I do know this, however: that lad that day was accessory to a miracle. I am not sure Jesus needed those five loaves and two fishes to do what he did — perhaps he could have done the same thing without them. But he used them, and this is the point — he used what the lad gave him, and of that little made much. So on that Galilean hillside that day that nameless lad became an accessory person, one of the Lord's helpers. Perhaps what he did wasn't much, but what he did helped.

Here is a good dictionary definition: "Accessory: an extra thing added to help something of more importance." In clothing, an accessory is some item which "goes with" the main garment to accent it, to "set it off," to help it, to assist it in achieving its finest effect. In any drama of human living, an accessory person is one who stands by and takes part in some way to help the act along. Not the main hero or heroine, the accessory person is not the one at the center of the spotlight, normally does not get the loudest applause, and usually is not much heralded in history. But the role of this person is essential in almost every good endeavor of humankind.

Now let me say this: in getting his work done in the world, God needs his accessory people. If I may, I want to be one of these — don't you? Perhaps neither you nor I can offer much; maybe our baskets contain no more than barley loaves and fishes — but in our Lord's hands our little can become his much. Our small accessory acts, our deeds of kindness, our words of love, may become building blocks of which are made the temple of God's glory in earth and at last in heaven.

Do you remember Moses? He was struggling to get the Israelites from Egypt to Canaan. On the way they encountered the

Amalekites, and at Rephidim a major battle was fought. While Joshua led the men of Israel on the battlefield, Moses climbed a nearby mountain and there lifted up his hands to God in prayer. While the hands of Moses were upraised, the battle surged in Israel's favor, but when his arms grew weary and his hands dropped to his side, the tide of battle each time turned the other way.

With Moses on the mountain were two men, Aaron and Hur. We know little about them — but there they were attending God's great man in that critical hour. At last, when the arms of Moses finally faltered, when he no longer had the strength to raise them again, these two men stood by him, the one on this side and the other on that, and while he prayed they held up his hands. By the day's end the Amalekites had been driven from the field, and the Israelites were a little farther along the way to their Promised Land.

In historical terms, Hur and Aaron were nobodys — Aaron we hear of on a few other occasions and Hur almost not at all. We remember them for this one thing: they upheld the hands of a great man. He was God's man, chosen and appointed, but his task was greater than his strength. Knowing this, his two friends were there when he needed them. Thank God for such people, for God's accessory persons — and for all who in the struggles for truth and beauty and good uphold the hands of the stalwart champions and who ultimately will not let them fail.

And, of course, there was Andrew — accessory person — the disciple who told Jesus about the lad in their midst that day in Galilee. Andrew was not a dramatic fellow, never an outstanding leader, never in the vanguard of movements. But he had a brother. And having met Jesus, Andrew went and sought that brother, and said to him, "We have found the Messiah," (John 1:41) and "he brought him to Jesus."

That brother's name was Simon; Jesus called him Peter, the "rock." After this, Andrew is not mentioned much in the narrative, but Peter is. Andrew could never be more than a simple follower — but oh, how devoted and how enthusiastic he was! He would never be one of the great among the disciples, but he brought one who would be among the very greatest.

You see, Andrew was one of God's accessory people. He was accessory to righteousness and the work of the Kingdom and the cause of Christ in the world. How wonderful to be a Saint Andrew type of person — as each of us can be. We may not be, like Peter, the kind of foundation rock upon which Christ can build a church, but we can be among the little pebbles that help to make up the mortar that holds the great stones of the structure together. And so are we among God's accessory people.

One of the accessory persons of the Bible with whom I am especially fascinated is another whose name we do not know. He was a poor man, I think, meaning that he had not much of this world's goods. His house was just inside Jerusalem's gate where the road came in from Bethany. He owned a young colt not yet "broken" for riding, and the colt was tied at the street's edge just outside his door. It was the beginning of the Passover, the first day of the week, early in the day. Two men came to his house and began to untie the colt, and he said, "Why?" They said, "The Lord needs him," and the poor man let him go.

Later that day, this man heard shouts coming from the city gate, and, looking, he saw a strange procession entering there. At the head of it was the most beautiful figure of man he had ever seen — and that man was riding upon his colt. People were scattering flowers along the way and waving branches of palm trees as that magnificent man came riding by — and his colt was walking placidly as though it had been ridden many times before. With what amazement the man must have stood and watched that procession pass, swelling within him, I think, some high-surging emotion no word could ever quite express.

Some great drama, he must have known, was reaching toward its climax, and he was an accessory in it. Its moment, its meaning, were too vast for him to comprehend at the time. Indeed for us today, as we stand in our accessory roles, the full magnitude of the present event, whatever it is, may be far beyond our own powers to perceive. But, with full understanding or without it, how great to be an accessory, making some kind of contribution to the triumphal march of Christ toward the glorious victories of his Kingdom!

In several important ways the greatest of all accessory people was John, the one known as the Baptizer, the man who presented Jesus as Messiah and Savior. John followed a long line of prophets, a thousand years of Hebrew prophecy. For most of that time the people had looked forward to the appearance of the Messiah, the coming of the Redeeming One. The prophets had spoken hopefully and longingly of his advent.

Then at last came John — out of the Jordanian wilderness. Jesus came and stood with him at the edge of the river there, and John said to the people, "This is He . . .! (John 1:30) "I am not worthy to untie his shoes," said John. "He will increase . . . I must decrease," John declared. I go — out and away — so that he may come — into his own. John was arrested, jailed, executed. And Jesus said that he was "more than a prophet," (Matthew 11:9) that "there has risen no one greater than John." (Matthew 11:11)

Some people do not make good accessories; they have to be in charge or they are unwilling to be in at all; they must play in the lead or they will play no role at all. We speak a lot about the qualities of leadership; but let me say that I believe the qualities of good accessoryship are equally important. And John had them. Sincerely he could say, "After me there comes one who ranks before me." (John 1:30) He could be content, having made the introduction, to bow off stage and see Another step into the spotlight — and so did he aid the work of Jesus at its beginning.

Much later, as Jesus was nearing the cross, worn and weary, he was one day in the house of Simon the Leper at Bethany (Matthew 26:6-13). Around him many were anxious and fearful and there was much coming and going. Into this assembly a certain woman came (we do not know her name), and entering the house of Simon, she approached Jesus carrying in her hands an alabaster jar of expensive ointment. This, without fanfare and in an impulsive act of utter devotion, she quietly poured over the head of Jesus as he sat in his place at a table.

Some of the disciples made an issue of it. The ointment could have been sold, they said, for a great deal of money; she had wasted the ointment, they argued. But Jesus said, "She has done a beautiful thing to me. In pouring this ointment on my body she has done it to prepare me for burial." No, alongside the awesome events that were taking shape around Jesus, this woman had not done much — just a little offering of ointment against the power of Rome, the blind anger of mobs, and the conspiracies of temple rulers. Not much had she done, but her simple act of thoughtful caring meant much to Jesus in that hour. There was not much, probably, that she could do, but what she could do she did, and Jesus praised her, giving her his thanks.

Two days later when they had whipped Jesus, put a crown of thorns on his brow, laid the cross on his back, and were forcing him up the slopes of Mount Golgotha, I am quite sure that mingled with the rancid odors of blood and sweat there was the sweet aroma of spikenard. And as that soothing aroma reached the nostrils of the suffering Christ he must have thought: among all this surging mass of hostile humanity there is someone who cares. And I think maybe, knowing this, the Master straightened his burning shoulders a little beneath their burden and, lifting his eyes toward Golgotha's summit, took new courage for going on. That woman, God bless her, was one of our Lord's accessory people, precious in his sight, important to him.

And consider for a moment the man Simon from Cyrene. He

was the one who, when Jesus, stumbling beneath the burden of the cross, was able to carry it no longer, assumed that burden for Jesus and carried it for him the rest of the way to the top of the mount.

Well, as long as our Lord still has work to do in the world, in a very real way he is still under the burden of that cross. Is there not something you and I can do to help? As long as there is sin to be overcome, evil to be purged away, darkness to be dispelled by light, so long does our Lord continue the struggle to achieve in our world that for which he came and died. Can we not join him in some way and somehow become accessories to truth and good and beauty? I think we can.

Not many of us will ever be great, but there is not one of us who cannot become an accessory to greatness. There may not be a great many tall-standing champions of righteousness, but there can be many who in common places and quiet ways give support to what is right over against the power of what is wrong. Not many can sit at the right hand and the left hand of the Lord in his Kingdom, but there are many who can at least be pages in his court.

In the work-a-day world of our common living it really is not hard at all to find some chance to be an accessory to the movement of humanity onward and upward, an accessory to life-at-its-best. Here, for example, is the gossip circle which gives you your chance to say, "I won't listen," your chance to discourage the irresponsible rumor by refusing it the credence of your attention. Here, for instance, is the gang that's running wild, and to it you can say, "I won't go; I won't run with you; I won't encourage this by my presence and participation." Or here is the instance of bitterness and bickering where persons are clawing at one another like angry cats. To these you can say, "I will not stoop to this; life is too short to be used up in such a way." Or perhaps there ahead of us is some brave person who dares to stand amid the fiery darts against the downpull, a champion for God and good. You can go and stand with that person; God help me to come and join you.

Yes, there was Andrew who came to Jesus in Galilee and said: There is a lad here — he has only five barley loaves and two small fishes, not much; but the lad is here — and his loaves and fishes are yours, Lord, if you can use them.

Andrew, be a messenger for me! Go tell the Master: there is a man here — or a woman, or a boy, or a girl; there is a person here, and this person is I. I have only a little to offer, but it's yours, Lord, if you can use it. I am ready, Master. I lift my basket with all that's in it, and I say, "Please take it, Lord, and use it if you can." Here am I, Lord, take me, and let me be somewhere, somehow one of your accessory people in this world.

How to Beat the High Cost of Living

Eleventh Sunday after Pentecost

"Labor . . .for the food which endures . . ." — *John 6:27*

Our Lord is concerned about the way in which we *use* our lives. When one has something in possession, it is important what use one makes of it. If you have a walking cane, you may use it to lean upon or you may use it as a weapon with which to strike your neighbor. If you have a hand at the end of your arm, you may open it and stroke the brow of a fevered child or you may close it into a fist and punch someone in the face. If you have an hour of time, you may possibly write a poem or you may possibly commit a murder.

Well, we have *life* — each of us perhaps 25,000 days of life altogether, maybe as much as 30,000. What will we do with it? How will we use it? Our Lord Christ is concerned about this. This much is certain: we are using it up; we are using up life. "Live it up!" somebody says. This is precisely what we are doing, each of us — we are living up life.

We talk a lot in our time about something called "the high cost of living." By this we mean so many dollars a week spent for food, so many dollars a month for car payments, so many dollars a year to buy a house, perhaps. And we rather generally agree that the "cost of living" is high. But let me tell you this: the dollars (or sheckels or marks or franks) which we pay out for food and clothing and shelter and all the other purchases we make — these are only the *attendant incidentals*. These dollar prices do not represent the "cost of living" at all. The actual *cost of our living* is much higher than the total of all such monetary expenditure, a great deal higher than we normally think.

How much does living really cost? How much will your living actually cost you? What amount of expenditure will you ultimately make in order to finish it and see it through? The answer is simple, clear, and undebatable: *Everything!* Your living will cost you everything, everything you've got or ever will have. It will cost you all you've earned or inherited — down to the last split second of your time, the last movement of a finger, the final flicker of an eyelash. All your dollars will one day belong to someone else, all your houses and lands, all the things you cherish now. Death is a part of the cost of living, its final installment, and in making that payment you will turn loose all of the things you are still holding when that time comes.

The cost of living is not payable in dollars only — for ultimately it will cost you all your time, all your strength, all your real and personal resources; you will spend everything you have. How long will it take? Who knows? Maybe thirty years, or sixty, or ninety — but the moment will come when all is spent. I do not know how much money you will spend on your next vacation or to have your house painted next summer, but I do know, when all is said and done, how much of everything you will have spent: *all of it*. Some of us may sometimes avoid some payments along the way, but the final payment is an all-inclusive one and is one we all must make.

For many years Borden Parker Bowne was professor of philosophy at Boston University. Once when he and his colleagues were discussing our increasing life-expectancy, Professor Bowne commented, "Yes, the life span is increasing, but one fact remains unchanged: the death rate is still once for each one of us." Yes, we are using up what we have, time is slipping away, strength is depleting, and somewhere out there we shall part with all of it. A relative of mine, having achieved considerable success in business and having decided at length to start spending some of the money he had been accumulating, said to me, "I have never seen a hearse with a U-Haul hooked on behind it!" I haven't either, have you?

Yes, death is surely a part of life; to be born into this world is to begin to die; to come into this world is to start the process of leaving it. In a very real sense, we die from what we have lived for. Willa Cather, in *Death Comes to the Archbishop*, has a young priest chide the old man for going out into bad weather without his warm clothing. The young man says, "You will catch your death of cold," and the old priest smilingly replies, "When I die it will not be of a cold, it will be from having lived!" And, my friend, when we really understand, we deeply know there is nothing wrong with doing that; there is, rather, a lot that's pretty wonderful about it.

There is the oft-told story of a certain fellow who was a confirmed and unmitigated hypochondriac, chronically complaining that he was ill, suffering from this malady or that. When at last he died and his body was taken out to the cemetery for burial, it was found that he already had his gravestone prepared, the inscription reading: "I told you I was sick!" He was, of course. So are we all. We are using ourselves up, consuming all we have, spending all we've got — and this is the first point I want to make: no matter how well we live, or how ill, our living will cost us everything.

At length, we will have *nothing* left. Nothing, that is, *unless* — unless we have converted something into *a spiritual quality that has abiding power*. And this is the second point I want to make: we *can* do this.

And, doing this, we have something that will still be ours; we can take it with us. But only that which is of spiritual value can be lastingly ours. And, likewise, the only thing we can lastingly leave to anybody else in this world is a heritage of spiritual value, beauty, truth, good, and love which we have managed somehow to get incorporated into the lives of others. All the material things which we might leave them will be just as temporary with them as they were with us; only the personally spiritual can be enduringly theirs, that which we have converted into values that last. And we *can* do this.

And so doing, we *can* beat the high cost of living. This is the only way we can do it: to take life's raw materials of time and thing and circumstance, intermix these with God's good grace, and from all of this produce the kind of personal and spiritual values that have surviving power in ourselves and others in this world and the next. Therefore, as Jesus says, "Do not labor for the food which perishes, but for the food which endures to eternal life." (John 6:27)

In 1 Corinthians, chapter 13, the Apostle Paul tells us that tongues will cease and knowledge pass away, but that faith, hope, and love abide — and that love never ends. He is saying to us that spiritual value has the capability of everlasting endurance. Thus, when, in the course of our living, we choose to go for what is spiritual, we have something powerful going for us, and neither time nor life nor death can ever take it away.

In Hebrews, chapter 12, we are told that the whole continuum of time is in process of removing what can be shaken so that what cannot be shaken may remain — therefore, let us use our life's resources in a quest for the unshakable things. You can't take it with you, someone says. Yes, you can — *if* you exchange it into the currency of the realm to which you are going. When physical life ends, the spiritual remains, but only that can remain which is, and the more spiritual the quality of your life the richer you will be.

The point is this: IF living is going to cost you everything — and it will — then why not invest the resources of life in that which has surviving quality? Want to beat the high cost of living? This is the only way you can do it — and this way you can. A primary privilege (and responsibility) of our living is to transform time, energy, and skill into a reservoir of spiritual vitality and power with residence in us and in others whose lives we have touched along the way.

A generating plant which manufactures electricity takes in coal and water from which steam is made by which generators are turned so that power flows out from the plant into the homes and shops of people in a wide area. Thus raw materials are converted into an energy that is of value in home and industry. You and I, likewise, are "generating plants" of a sort. We take into our lives the raw materials of time and circumstance, and our assignment is to produce from these something of worth in our lives and the lives of persons all around us in the present and in days to come.

This some people do — to the blessing of humankind. And some do not. There are folks, sadly, who use up all they have, never producing anything that matters, anything that adds to the world's enduring wealth of the good and the lovely and the true. They pay out the full price down to the final farthing, and for it all there is nothing to show at the last.

In a small mid-American city I know well, lived a thirty-six-year-old loafer, a kind of town bum who had never done anything productive in his life, who had never tried, and apparently had never cared. Inheriting $2,200 from an uncle, he bought a jug of wine, went into a small garage and machine shop at the south edge of town, sat down on the floor, leaned back against the wall, and drank the wine. His half-drunken buddies brought him other jugs, keeping him supplied day and night. For eight days and nights that young man sat there on that floor in his drunkenness and filth. He never moved from that place; and there at age thirty-six, sitting on that floor, leaning against that wall, after eight days he died. There he peeled out the last frayed yards of life's long rope, there to the last dregs he emptied life's once-brimming cup, and it was all over. He had used up all there was.

Good people of the neighborhood took his body out to Kirkwood Cemetery and put it in the ground — and what was left? What did he leave behind? What remained of him in the life of the world, in the lives of other persons? Nothing but bruises and scars and abrasions and running sores and broken things. And what did he have to take with him? He had spent all of life there was, he had flung down on the bargaining counter every precious sheckel of its silver and gold, and all was gone. He had taken all that God and life and a free country and a good community could give him, and from it all he had produced nothing of any ultimate worth to himself or anyone else.

To find an illustration of a life well-invested and wisely used, one might turn in any one of a thousand directions, for many persons have done this with their lives, and a good number of their names are boldly inscribed on the honor rolls of history. Let us look at just one, William Booth, the inimitable founder of the Salvation Army. When he died in London in 1912, a British newspaper published two pictures on its front page, the one of William Booth and the other of a society matron who had died the same day. The printed caption was this: "The woman lived one life and had a thousand dresses; the man William Booth had one suit and lived a thousand lives." There is good reason to say what Jesus said: Do not labor for what perishes, but for what endures.

Too many people spend too much for too little; their lives are used up in pursuit of what is not worth pursuing; they are consumed, burned out, on trifles. They wear themselves away over what is not worth the price they pay. Here, for instance, is a woman who says, "I am having so much trouble." She appears harried and distraught, and I think: what is this awful condition which has come upon her? It may be that she is all "put out" with another woman over some trifle at the card club. Or here is the woman who is emotionally upset, drained, and depressed, and I think: what is this tragic circumstance? It may be that she had spent considerable time shopping for just the right dress and then, having found and bought it, discovered that one of her acquaintances has one exactly like it. Or here is a man who is nervous and exhausted, growling like a tiger at all around him, impossible to please in anything, smoking twice as many cigarettes as usual, and I think: what terrible calamity has befallen him? It may be that he has not received the invitation he wanted to become a member of the city's most exclusive club.

Too bad, isn't it, that we should use up our lives, exhaust and deplete ourselves, and then have nothing to show for the exhaustion except a few trinkets and trifles. And certainly it is a major calamity and waste when the resources of our lives are burned out on resentment, hate, or bickering, when life is all used up in building barriers, the kind of walls behind which people sulk and pout and from which they peer out and hurl their brickbats. Living is costing each of us so much that it's the very poorest of stewardship to expend our precious resources of mind and spirit, of strength and time, on trifles that do not really matter or troubles that we manufacture for ourselves. Troubles enough we have already — of the uninvited kind.

Let us rid ourselves of the burdens we needlessly bear and try to save our strength for bearing the ones we must. How, you ask, can we do this? Probably more easily than you think. Let me suggest some burden-lifting exercises — try them, and you'll be surprised how well they work.

Maybe you have been involved in a running feud with some fellow who years ago offended you in some way and you reacted to the offense and he reacted to your reaction, and he and you have been at swordpoints ever since. Today perhaps you cannot even remember what the issues are between the two of you, but you try to avoid this fellow as much as you can, and when you cannot, you find yourself saying and doing stinging little things to hurt him; you really cannot tell how much they hurt, but you know that you are hurting, and you hope only that he is hurting more. And you know that all the while he is doing similar things to you. Well, at your very next opportunity, walk up to this man, put your hand on his shoulder, look him in the eye, and say, "It's just not worth it, brother; let's be men — and friends again."

I cannot guarantee how this man will react to this, nor can you. But whatever his response may be, I know this: in doing what you have done, you have divested yourself of a burden, you have gotten free of a chain that bound you; you have cut yourself loose from a problem that had drained away your strength — and now, at least in this quarter of what you are — you are free to live again.

Maybe there is a woman whose every word and act for a long time has been nothing but one interminable irritation to you; the whole current of her life has seemed to be at crosscurrents with yours. Reach out in firm handclasp and say, "It isn't worth it, sister."

Or maybe in your marriage there has been a drifting away, until lately each little thing has become a distressing irritation. Your days are taken up with an edgy insecurity that makes you always weary and brings you at each day's close to a point of utter fatigue. Well, do this, my friend: take in tender embrace that partner of yours and say, "Our lives are too precious, our days too few, to use them up this way; it just isn't worth it, dear; we are paying too much to realize so little — what do you say we back up and start over?"

Sometimes, often, really, along life's way we drift into quagmires, we stumble into quicksands, and sometimes we use up our lives just wallowing there. What a waste! Once in a while we need to look in a mirror, see ourselves as we are, and ask: Is my life going for something worth it? It *is* going, my life — no question about that. But for what? Day by day, I am using it up. I am putting all of its raw materials through a process, and what is the result, what will the product be? What am I making out of what is given me?

I can tell you this: you *can* make something beautiful. Whoever you are, under whatever conditions you live, you can produce a spiritual and personal worth that nothing can ever destroy, that no one can ever take away. You can develop gem-like qualities of spirit that become treasures in heaven, where, as Jesus says, "neither moth nor rust consumes and where thieves do not break in and steal" (Matthew 6:20).

Yes, the cost of living is high. But, ah, life is worth the cost! My living will cost me everything. But, thank God, I have found the way to beat my living's high cost: I can invest my life's resources of time and strength to produce spiritual dividends that will endure forever. When all my capital has been used up, the dividends will still be mine! When time and strength are gone, love and faith will be lasting on. So I will choose to use my 30,000 days in such ways that, by God's good grace, I will have a treasure that is precious, priceless, and permanent. Jesus says the fruits of labor may be one of two, that which perishes or that which endures — and I choose the latter. And when I shall have paid the full price for my privilege of living, I shall have received and gained far more than my living ever cost me.

Our Most Extravagant Giver

Twelfth Sunday after Pentecost

"I am the bread of life . . ." — *John 6:48*

The art of giving is one not often mastered. In much so-called giving there is an element of barter, but giving, to be true, must be barter-free. A true gift is not a pay-off for past favors nor a bribe for future ones; it must be tendered from worthy motives and in a spirit which is right. It is more than the mere transfer of some thing from one pair of hands to another; it is rather the transfer of a part of one person into another person; it is not merely an exercise of the hand, but of the heart. As writes James Russell Lowell in the *Vision of Sir Launfal*, "The gift without the giver is bare."

History's most perfect epitome of real giving is expressed in these oft-quoted words of John 3:16: "God so loved the world that he gave . . ." Here is the quintessence of giving. Here the gift is not a thing apart from the giver; he comes with his gift, he is in it, and it is he. "God was in Christ . . ." (2 Corinthians 5:19) and "My Father and I are one . . ." (John 10:30) Nor is this Gift of God some worthless trinket or surplus item he could easily spare — as our so-called gifts sometimes are: God's gift was his own and only Son, heaven's best, what we needed most.

So it is quite logical that Jesus should say what he says in John 6: "I am the bread which came down from heaven . . . I am the bread of life." Bread is an essential. Jesus did not say: I am the pie-a-la-mode of life, or the pineapple upsidedown cake, or the chocolate ice cream; he said, "I am the bread." What he is to our human spirits is as essential as bread is to our human bodies. We may get along without pie or cake or ice cream, but bread is the "staff" of our physical well-being — the very word is a synonym for food in general, without which our physical bodies would starve and die. Thus, what the heavenly Father is offering to us in Christ is not a frill or an option, but for our highest good it is an *essential*, a necessity — as necessary as bread is.

In the second place, what God is providing in Christ is enduring, it is *lasting*. The Hebrew forefathers ate manna in the wilderness, and they died; they did not die because the manna was lethal, but because their bodies were mortal. But Jesus, depicting himself as the bread of life, tells us that he is not the physical kind which grows up from the ground, but is that of spiritual quality which comes down from heaven, of which, if one eats, he shall not die. Although the manna-fed body shall pass away, the spirit-fed soul shall live on.

In the third place, what God is providing in Christ is indeed a *gift*. What the Father did in sending his Son was voluntary — no force compelled him to do it; it was his choice because he cared, because he loved. And it was unconditional — he gave his Son without any reservations with respect to how we would receive him or treat him. God did not send a survey team in advance to find out what sort of reception he would have in our midst. God did not send out a team of pollsters to determine how many would be for him and how many against him. God did not say: now if you humans will do so and so, I will send my Son — he just sent him.

And when Jesus came there is no record that he ever held any negotiating sessions with Caiaphas and Pilate and the Sanhedrin before he would consent to declare himself as the Messiah and the Savior of the world: he just did it. The coming of Christ was in fact a true gift of the heavenly Father to the world.

When God gives a gift there are never any attached strings by which he may yank it back. No matter how his gifts are received, when received, they are for keeps. For example, when he gives pardon for our sins, he buries them to the depth of the sea and never brings them up again. Although today's offenses may hurt him deeply, he never withdraws the forgiveness he granted for the sins of yesterday. Our God is a giver — in the true meaning of that word.

And he is a most *extravagant* giver. So generous! In great profusion to us his gifts come. The psalmist said it this way: "Thou has multiplied, O Lord my God, thy wondrous deeds and thy thoughts toward us; none can compare with thee! Were I to proclaim and tell of them, they would be more than can be numbered." (Psalm 40:5)

The abundances of God are everywhere to be seen. In nature, for instance, the seeds of his growing plants are blown in the winds, floated on the waters, carried about by insects and birds, and they lodge among the rocks, fall into the sands or seas, but every once in a while one of these takes root and grows. And there is the immensity of his mountains, the expanse of his seas, the multitude of his stars, the awesome dimensions of his space. There are the coal under the mountains, the diamonds deep in the earth, and the beauty of things — the colors and shapes of them. There is the extravaganza of a sunset where God usually seems to use a lot more clouds than he really needs. There is the glory of a sunrise; and, as the planets wheel, the journey of the sun across the sky. There is the blooming of flowers in garden and wilderness, on mountain summits, amid desert rocks, across vast swamplands, and everywhere.

It was Thomas Gray who wrote that "many a rose blooms to blush unseen and waste its fragrance on the desert air." Waste? I wonder if it is, for perhaps God himself enjoys the fragrance of a rose — and never does one bloom where God is not. Perhaps God enjoys the same sights we do and the music his whole creation makes. Someone has thoughtfully said that there are three elemental sounds in the earth: the sound of rain, the sound of wind in the primeval wood, and the sound of the outer ocean where it meets the shore. And sometimes I have thought when I have stood alone out there that God and I were enjoying it together.

But the remarkable extravaganza of God's handiwork in natural creation does not end with what we can see — it also has fantastic form beyond the normal reach of our sight. Down in the microscopic and sub-microscopic world of design and pattern and out into vast, imponderable distances where no telescope can probe, here God has provided his abundances also — everywhere immense profusions of things, all the way from the heart of an atom to the magnificent rings of Saturn. Occasionally in the motion picture industry we hear talk of a "movie spectacular" or a "movie extravaganza." Well, such films are as nothing in comparison with the extravaganza of our Lord in his natural order of things.

All of this, though, is merely an illustration of what we want to talk about. We want to think here of God's extravagant giving in other dimensions of our life's exposure and experience. It is not in nature only that we see God as an extravagant giver; we see his abundances elsewhere also. We see them especially, if we look, in the realm of spirit and mind, and most notably in his redemptive reach for us in Jesus Christ and through his Spirit.

We are told that on a mountainside in Galilee Jesus fed 5,000 people with five barley loaves and two small fishes. The amazing thing is that when all had "eaten their fill" there were gathered up twelve baskets full of the fragments that were left. Usually when a big dinner is reported in the news not much is said concerning the clean-up operation. But to me the clean-up part of this story is one of the best parts of it. It is saying to me that there was an over-abundance of food; nobody went away hungry; there was plenty for every one, and to spare. It is saying to me that God is not only a doer — he is an *overdoer*! There is nothing miserly about our Lord; he does things in a big way.

The psalmist knew this. In his hungerings and thirstings of spirit, he searched to discover God's way with humankind. What he found was a God whose gifts are showered upon his people in wild and wonderful profusion. The Book of Psalms is a book of superlatives. Here is the portrait of a God who satisfies and fills the human spirit in ways beyond the wildest dream, a God to whom highest praise is due, to whom supreme thanks should be given.

The magnificent Twenty-third Psalm is a psalm of abundance — the Lord is not merely good; he is very, very good. As a shepherd, he leads his sheep not into just any pasture, but into pastures green, not just to any watering-place, but to waters that are still. And when the psalm writer lifts his cup in the hope that the Lord will pour into it some trickle of blessing, suddenly he utters the joyful shout, "My cup runs over!" His cup was not merely filled; it was (almost wastefully it would seem to us) over-filled. This is the way the psalmist found God to be, a lavish giver, richly outpouring his goodness and loving care in measure far beyond simple requirements and common minimums.

This is also the way the Apostle Paul understands God. In Ephesians 3:20 he declares that God "is able to do far more abundantly than all we ask or think." As Paul sees it, God's forgiveness of our sins is not a favor grudgingly given, but is given generously "according to the riches of his grace which he lavished upon us." (Ephesians 1:7, 8) He writes excitedly of "the immeasurable greatness of (God's) power in us who believe, according to the working of his great might," (Ephesians 1:19) and of "the immeasurable riches of his grace in kindness toward us in Christ Jesus." (Ephesians 2:7) He says that "where sin abounded, grace did much more abound" or "where sin increased, grace abounded all the more." (Romans 5:20) In hearty praise of him, Paul writes of "God who richly furnishes us with everything to enjoy," (1 Timothy 6:17) and he boldly says, "My God will supply every need of yours according to his riches in glory in Christ Jesus." (Philippians 4:19)

Like the psalmist, Paul is saying, "My cup runneth over!" And if you and I can understand God as Paul and the psalmist did, we too can know that what our Lord offers to us is available in such overflowing abundance that we also may say, "My cup runneth over." Our God is not bankrupt so that he should find it necessary to dole out the goodies of his grace in microscopic morsels! Nor is he stingy so that he should want to keep it all for himself! Our God is a giver — in the true sense of giving — and he is an extravagant one.

Do you remember the "prodigal son" in the parable Jesus told? After he had wandered about for a while, had wasted all his money, and was destitute and hungry, at last "he came to himself" and said, "In my father's house there is bread enough, and to spare." And, friend, you and I need to realize and appreciate the wealth of our heavenly Father's house. the prodigal thought that if he went home perhaps he could expect the treatment of a hired servant. But look what happened. When his father saw him coming he ran and met him and kissed him and led him into the main dining room and killed the "fatted calf" — and that boy's return to his home became the social event of the season! What the father stood ready to give was many times more than the son had any reason to hope for.

Do you recall what Jesus said about the rooms in his Father's house? As recorded in John 14, Jesus was telling his disciples about what was being prepared for them in the future. He was saying, Do not be troubled, believe. Then he said, "In my Father's house are many rooms." The King James Version of 1611 had it this way: "In my Father's house are many mansions." We normally think of a mansion as being larger than a house, so in later translations the word became "rooms," for how can you expect to put many larger things into a single smaller one? For this reason, the more recent translations are more logical, more in line with our normal expectations.

We need to remember, however, that what God provides is not always limited to what is logical or restricted to what we expect. Sometimes he goes beyond logic, far beyond; sometimes our expectations are juvenile gestures in comparison with what he stands ready to deliver. Anyway, rooms in a house — or mansions? The Greek word means "abiding-places," living-places, if you please — not just little cubicles to sit in, but wide spaces to live in, with provision for all that living is. And the Lord Christ declares there are many of them. God has not provided cramped quarters for a few, but ample place for multitudes; our Father's house is extravagantly furnished. And such is the prospect for our future.

Then, too, in the very present struggles of our lives, amid the perils of current time, we can know that the abundances of God are outpoured to the overflowing in our behalf. The writer of the New Testament Epistle of James lived in a time of much suffering. The Christians were under persecution; there was the unrelenting pressure of mighty evils, the crushing weight of a general hostility. It was a difficult and exhausting time; some of the Lord's followers were falling away, and others, under tensions, were fighting among themselves. In writing his letter James recognizes all of this, but he also sees another element in the picture. The people are not alone in their struggles; God is there with them, and, says James, "He gives more grace." (James 4:6)

The problems of God's people may pile up like mountains — but he gives more grace, more of what it takes to match them. The pressures may mount — but he gives more grace. The difficulties may accumulate — but he gives more grace. God always has a ready reserve to provide for us more than we need. "Ask and it will be given you," said Jesus. (Matthew 7:7) It was with good reason that John wrote to his persecuted friends of the primitive Church, "He who is in you is greater than he who is in the world." (1 John 4:4) Yes, now and forever, our Lord is a generous provider, an extravagant giver. And it is appropriate, and altogether consistent with God's extravagant manner, that Jesus should come to us saying, "I am the bread which came down from heaven . . . I am the bread of life."

I went to the dictionary to find the meaning of the word "extravagant." Reading the definition, the first words I saw were these: *"Going beyond the bounds of reason."* Is it not this which our Lord is always doing? Isn't he forever, and in so many ways, going beyond the bounds of reason?

Looking at humanity, I suspect God had good reason to wipe us off this planet long ago; but he didn't. He loved us, and where love is, reason alone cannot rule. When reason says patience and compassion must end, love says: Not yet. Thus, "God so loves that he gives . . ." In spite of our sins (yes, because of them), God gives. The Christ comes, the Holy Spirit is given — *and the bounds of reason are broken*.

We commit our trespasses and our sins against our Lord, and the Christ comes to us and we come to him. For his sake we are forgiven — and the bounds of reason are broken again — and again — and again.

One cannot experience the whole thrill of a sunset by knowledge of pure science, without feeling and without heart. Neither can we ever understand compassion, forgiveness, and mercy by the rules of logic alone. Our Lord is our most extravagant giver, giving beyond the bounds of reason — we must never lose this truth. And if you and I are ever to know him as he is, we must experience that knowledge by the exercise of an extravagant faith, a faith which, like God's giving, goes beyond the bounds of reason.

The gifts of God to us are not limited to what we may reasonably expect of him; and often we do not see or receive them because they are so much greater than anything we are prepared to look for. He is offering to us in glorious profusion his abundances of love and grace and forgiveness and peace and power, and he is trying to get us to receive them. He is trying to give us as much as we are willing to receive, as much as we have the openness and faith to accept. He makes his offers, amazing and wonderful — but let us remember: only what is received can be given, really; it is only by acceptance of an offered gift that the transaction is made. And God awaits our acceptance of the precious and priceless gift extravaganza that he offers.

We commenced this sermon saying that giving is an art not often mastered. We conclude it saying there is an art in receiving also. Properly to receive a gift, we need some awareness of its worth, some sense of thankfulness that it is ours, some feeling of gratitude to the giver, and some perception of its meaning in our future. To receive the abounding gifts of God, we need, by faith, to stretch our perceptions widely. And, by faith, we can.

Jesus said, "I am the bread." In the sacrament of Holy Communion we understand that he is the bread "given" for us. What is said in the Sacrament let me now say sincerely and prayerfully to you: "TAKE — THE BREAD."